CONTENTS

GENERAL INTRODUCTION

THE PLAY

APPENDICES

ACKNOWLEDGEMENTS

My grateful thanks to all who have helped in the growth and development of this work. Special thanks to Norman Welsh who first introduced me to the Folio Text, and to Tina Packer who (with Kristin Linklater and all the members of Shakespeare & Co.) allowed me to explore the texts on the rehearsal floor. To Jane Nichols for her enormous generosity in providing the funding which allowed the material to be computerised. To James and Margaret McBride and Terry Lim for their expertise, good humour and hard work. To the National Endowment for the Arts for their award of a Major Artist Fellowship and to York University for their award of the Joseph G. Green Fellowship. To actors, directors and dramaturgs at the Stratford Festival, Ontario; Toronto Free Theatre (that was); the Skylight Theatre, Toronto and Tamanhouse Theatre of Vancouver. To colleagues, friends and students at The University of British Columbia, Vancouver; York University, Toronto; Concordia University, Montreal; The National Theatre School of Canada in Montreal; Equity Showcase Theatre, Toronto; The Centre for Actors Study and Training (C.A.S.T.), Toronto; The National Voice Intensive at Simon Fraser University, Vancouver; Studio 58 of Langara College, Vancouver; Professional Workshops in the Arts, Vancouver; U.C.L.A., Los Angeles; Loyola Marymount, Los Angeles; San Jose State College, California; Long Beach State College, California; Brigham Young University, Utah, and Hawaii; Holy Cross College, Massachussetts; Guilford College, North Carolina. To Chairman John Wright and Associate Dean Don Paterson for their incredible personal support and encouragement. To Rachel Ditor and Tom Scholte for their timely research assistance. To Alan and Chris Baker, and Stephanie McWilliams for typographical advice. To Jay L. Halio, Hugh Richmond, and G.B. Shand for their critical input. To the overworked and underpaid proofreading teams of Ron Oten and Yuuattee Tanipersaud, Patrick Galligan and Leslie Barton, Janet Van De Graaff and Angela Dorhman (with input from Todd Sandomirsky, Bruce Alexander Pitkin, Catelyn Thornton and Michael Roberts). And above all to my wife Julie, for her patient encouragement, courteous advice, critical eye and long sufferance!

SPECIAL ACKNOWLEDGEMENTS

Glenn Young and Paul Sugarman of Applause Books; Houghton Mifflin Company for permission to quote from the line numbering system developed for *The Riverside Shakespeare*: Evans, Gwynne Blakemore, Harry Levin, Anne Barton, Herschel Baker, Frank Kermode, Hallet D. Smith, and Marie Edel, editors, *The Riverside Shakespeare*. Copyright © 1974 by Houghton Mifflin Company.

APPLAUSE FIRST FOLIO EDITIONS

The Life and Death of King John

BY

William Shakespeare

PREPARED & ANNOTATED BY

NEIL FREEMAN

The Applause Shakespeare Library
Folio Texts
AN APPLAUSE ORIGINAL

The Life and Death of King John

original concept devised by Neil Freeman

original research computer entry by Margaret McBride

original software programmes designed and developed by
James McBride and Terry Lim

Text layout designed and executed by Neil Freeman

Some elements of this text were privately published under the collective title of
The Freeman–Nichols Folio Scripts 1991–96

Copyright ° 2000 by Folio Scripts, Vancouver, Canada

ISBN: 1-55783-383-4

Library of Congress Cataloging-in-Publication Data

Library of Congress Catalog Card Number: 00-103946

British Library Cataloging-in-Publication Data

A catalogue record of this book is available from the British Library

APPLAUSE BOOKS

1841 Broadway Suite 1100	Combined Book Services Ltd.
New York, NY 10023	Units I/K Paddock Wood Dist. Ctr.
Phone (212) 765-7880	Paddock Wood,
Fax: (212) 765-7875	Tonbridge Kent TN12 6UU
	Phone 0189 283-7171
	Fax 0189 283-7272

Printed in Canada

DEFINITIONS OF AND GUIDE TO PHOTOGRAPHIC COPIES OF THE EARLY TEXTS

(see Appendix A for a brief history of the First Folio, the Quartos, and their uneasy relationship with modern texts)

A QUARTO (Q)

A single text, so called because of the book size resulting from a particular method of printing. Eighteen of Shakespeare's plays were published in this format by different publishers at various dates between 1594–1622 prior to the appearance of the 1623 Folio. Of the eighteen quarto texts, scholars suggest that fourteen have value as source texts. An extremely useful collection of them is to be found in Michael J. B. Allen and Kenneth Muir, eds., *Shakespeare's Plays in Quarto* (Berkeley: University of California Press, 1981).

THE FIRST FOLIO (F1)[1]

Thirty-six of Shakespeare's plays (excluding *Pericles* and *Two Noble Kinsmen,* in which he had a hand) appeared in one volume published in 1623. All books of this size were termed Folios, again because of the sheet size and printing method, hence this volume is referred to as the First Folio; two recent photographic editions of the work are:

Charlton Hinman, ed., *The Norton Facsimile (The First Folio of Shakespeare)* (1968; republished New York: W. W. Norton & Company, Inc., 1996).

Helge Kökeritz, ed., *Mr. William Shakespeare's Comedies, Histories & Tragedies* (New Haven: Yale University Press, 1954).

THE SECOND FOLIO (F2)

Scholars suggest that the Second Folio, dated 1632 but perhaps not published until 1640, has little authority, especially since it created hundreds of new problematical readings of its own. Nevertheless, more than eight hundred modern text readings can be attributed to it. The most recent reproduction is D. S. Brewer, ed., *Mr.*

---

[1] For a full overview of the First Folio see the monumental two-volume work: Charlton Hinman, *The Printing and Proof Reading of the First Folio of Shakespeare* (2 volumes) (Oxford: Clarendon Press, 1963) and W. W. Greg, *The Editorial Problem in Shakespeare: a Survey of the Foundations of the Text,* 3rd. ed. (Oxford: Clarendon Press, 1954); for a brief summary, see the forty-six page publication from Peter W. M. Blayney, *The First Folio of Shakespeare* (Washington, DC: Folger Library Publications, 1991).

William Shakespeare's Comedies, Histories & Tragedies, the Second Folio Reproduced in Facsimile (Dover, NH: Boydell & Brewer Ltd., 1985).

The Third Folio (1664) and the Fourth Folio (1685) have even less authority, and are rarely consulted except in cases of extreme difficulty.

THE THIRD FOLIO (F3)

The Third Folio, carefully proofed (though apparently not against the previous edition) takes great pains to correct anomalies in punctuation ending speeches and in expanding abbreviations. It also introduced seven new plays supposedly written by Shakespeare, only one of which, *Pericles*, has been established as such. The most recent reproduction is D. S. Brewer, ed., *Mr. William Shakespeare's Comedies, Histories & Tragedies, the Third Folio Reproduced in Facsimile* (Dover, NH: Boydell & Brewer Ltd., 1985).

THE FOURTH FOLIO (F4)

Paradoxically, while the Fourth Folio was the most carefully edited of all, its concentration on grammatical clarity and ease of comprehension by its readers at the expense of faithful reproduction of F1 renders it the least useful for those interested in the setting down on paper of Elizabethan theatre texts. The most recent reproduction is D. S. Brewer, ed., *Mr. William Shakespeare's Comedies, Histories & Tragedies, the Fourth Folio Reproduced in Facsimile* (Dover, NH: Boydell & Brewer Ltd., 1985).

WELCOME TO THESE SCRIPTS

These scripts are designed to do three things:

1. show the reader what the First Folio (often referred to as F1) set down on paper, rather than what modern editions think ought to have been set down

2. provide both reader and theatre practitioner an easy journey through some of the information the original readers might have garnered from F1 and other contemporary scripts which is still relevant today

3. provide a simple way for readers to see not only where modern texts alter the First Folio, and how, but also allow readers to explore both First Folio and modern versions of the disputed passage without having to turn to an Appendix or a different text

all this, hopefully without interfering with the action of the play.

What the First Folio sets on paper will be the basis for what you see. In the body of the play-text that follows, the words (including spellings and capitalisations), the punctuation (no matter how ungrammatical), the structure of the lines (including those moments of peculiar verse or unusual prose), the stage directions, the act and scene divisions, and (for the most part) the prefixes used for each character will be as set in the First Folio.

In addition, new, on page, visual symbols specially devised for these texts will help point out both the major stepping stones in the Elizabethan debate/rhetorical process contained in the plays (a fundamental part of understanding both the inner nature of each character as well as the emotional clashes between them), and where and how (and sometimes why) modern texts have altered the First Folio information. And, unlike any other script, opposite each page of text will be a blank page where readers can make their own notes and commentary.

However, there will be the rare occasion when these texts do not exactly follow the First Folio.

Sometimes F1's **words or phrases** are meaningless; for example, the lovely misprinting of 'which' in *Twelfth Night* as 'wh?ch', or in *Romeo and Juliet* the typesetting corruptions of 'speeh' for 'speech' and the running of the two words 'not away' as 'notaway'. If there are no alternative contemporary texts (a Quarto version of the play) or if no modification was made by any of the later Folios (The Second Folio of 1632, The Third Folio of 1664, or The Fourth Folio of 1685, termed F2, F3, and F4 respectively) then the F1 printing will be set as is, no matter how peculiar, and the modern correction footnoted. However, if a more appropriate alternative is available in a Quarto (often referred to as Q) or F2, F3, or F4, that 'correction' will be set directly into the text, replacing the F1 reading, and footnoted accordingly, as in the case of 'wh?ch', 'speeh', and 'notaway'.

The only time F1's **punctuation** will be altered is when the original setting is so blurred that an accurate deciphering of what F1 set cannot be determined. In such cases, alternative punctuation from F2–4 or Q will be set and a footnote will explain why.

The only time F1's **line structure** will not be followed is when at the end of a very long line, the final word or part of the word cannot fit onto the single line, nor be set as a new line in F1 because of the text that follows and is therefore set above or below the original line at the right hand side of the column. In such rare cases these texts will complete the line as a single line, and mark it with a † to show the change from F1. In all other cases, even when in prose F1 is forced to split the final word of a speech in half, and set only a few letters of it on a new line—for example in *Henry the Fifth*, Pistoll's name is split as 'Pi' on one line and 'stoll' (as the last part of the speech) on the next—these texts will show F1 exactly as set.

Some liberties have to be taken with the **prefixes** (the names used at the beginning of speeches to show the reader which character is now speaking), for Ff (all the Folios) and Qq (all the Quartos) are not always consistent. Sometimes slightly different abbreviations are used for the same character—in *The Tempest*, King Alonso is variously referred to as 'Al.', 'Alo.', 'Alon.', and 'Alonso'. Sometimes the same abbreviation is used for two different characters—in *A Midsummer Nights Dream* the characters Quince, the 'director' and author of the Mechanicals play, and Titania, Queen of the fairies, are given the same abbreviation 'Qu.'. While in this play common sense can distinguish what is intended, the confusions in *Julius Caesar* between Lucius and Lucullus, each referred to sometimes as 'Luc.', and in *The Comedy of Errors*, where the twin brothers Antipholus are both abbreviated to 'Antiph.', cannot be so easily sorted out. Thus, whereas F1 will show a variety of abbreviated prefixes, these texts will usually choose just one complete name per character and stay with it throughout.

However, there are certain cases where one full name will not suffice. Sometimes F1 will change the prefix for a single character from scene to scene, the change usually reflecting the character's new function or status. Thus in *The Comedy of Errors*, as a drinking companion of the local Antipholus, the goldsmith Angelo is referred to by his given name 'Ang.', but once business matters go awry he very quickly becomes a businessman, referred to as 'Gold'. Similar changes affect most of the characters in *A Midsummer Nights Dream*, and a complex example can be found in *Romeo and Juliet*. While modern texts give Juliet's mother the single prefix Lady Capulet throughout (incorrectly since neither she nor Capulet are named as aristocrats anywhere in the play) both Ff and Qq refer to her in a wonderful character-revealing multiplicity of ways—Mother, Capulet Wife, Lady, and Old Lady—a splendid gift for actress, director, designer, and reader alike.

Surprisingly, no modern text ever sets any of these variations. Believing such changes integral to the development of the characters so affected, these texts will. In such cases, each time the character's prefix changes the new prefix will be set, and a small notation alongside the prefix (either by reference to the old name, or by adding the symbol •) will remind the reader to whom it refers.

Also, some alterations will be made to F1's **stage directions,** not to the words themselves or when they occur, but to the way they are going to be presented visually. Scholars agree F1 contains two different types of stage direction: those that came in the original manuscript from which the Playhouse copy of the play was made, and a second set that were added in for theatrical clarification by the Playhouse. The scholars conjecture that the literary or manuscript directions, presumably from Shakespeare, mainly dealing with entries and key actions such as battles, are those that F1 sets centred on a separate line, while the additional Playhouse directions, usually dealing with offstage sounds, music, and exits, are those F1 sets alongside the spoken dialogue, usually flush against the right hand side of the column. In performance terms there seems to be a useful distinction between the two, though this is only a rule of thumb. The centred manuscript (Shakespearean?) directions tend to stop or change the action of the play, that is, the scene is affected by the action the direction demands, whereas the Playhouse directions (to the side of the text) serve to underscore what is already taking place. (If a word is needed to distinguish the two, the centred directions can be called 'action' directions, because they are events in and of themselves, while the side-set directions could be called 'supportive' or 'continuous' since they tend not to distract from the current onstage action.)

Since F1 seems to visually distinguish between the two types (setting them on different parts of the page) and there seems to be a logical theatrical differentiation as to both the source and function of each, it seems only appropriate that these scripts also mark the difference between them. Both Ff and Qq's side-set directions are often difficult to decipher while reading the text: sometimes they are set so close to the spoken text they get muddled up with it, despite the different typeface, and oftentimes have to be abbreviated to fit in. These are drawbacks shared by most modern texts. Thus these texts will distinguish them in a slightly different way (see p. xxvi below).

Finally, there will be two occasional alterations to Ff's **fonts.** F1 used **italics** for a large number of different purposes, sometimes creating confusion on the page. What these texts will keep as italics are letters, poems, songs, and the use of foreign languages. What they will not set in italics are real names, prefixes, and stage directions. Also at the top of each play, and sometimes at the beginning of a letter or poem, F1 would set a large wonderfully **decorative opening letter,** with the second letter of the word being capitalised, the style tying in with the borders that surrounded the opening and closing of each play. Since these texts will not be reproducing the decorative borders, the decorative letters won't be set either.

MAKING FULL USE OF THESE TEXTS

WHAT MODERN CHANGES WILL BE SHOWN

WORDS AND PHRASES

Modern texts often tidy up F1's words and phrases. Real names, both of people and places, and foreign languages are often reworked for modern understanding; for example, the French town often set in F1 as 'Callice' is usually reset as 'Calais'. Modern texts 'correct' the occasional Elizabethan practice of setting a singular noun with plural verb (and vice versa), as well as the infrequent use of the past tense of a verb to describe a current situation. These texts will set the F1 reading, and footnote the modern corrections whenever they occur.

More problematical are the possibilities of choice, especially when a Q and F version of the same play show a different reading for the same line and either choice is valid—even more so when both versions are offered by different modern texts. Juliet's 'When I shall die,/Take him and cut him out in little starres' offered by Ff/Q1-3 being offset by Q4's 'When he shall die...' is a case in point. Again, these texts will set the F1 reading, and footnote the alternatives.

LINE STRUCTURE CHANGES RELATED TO PROBLEMS OF 'CASTING-OFF'

The First Folio was usually prepared in blocks of twelve pages at a time. Six pairs of pages would be prepared, working both forward and backward simultaneously. Thus from the centre of any twelve-page block, pages six and seven were set first, then five and eight, then four and nine, then three and ten, then two and eleven, and finally one and twelve. This meant each compositor had to work out very carefully how much copy would fit not only each sheet, but also how much would be needed overall to reach the outer edges of pages one and twelve to match it to the previously set text, (prior to page one) or about to be set text (after page twelve). Naturally the calculations weren't always accurate. Sometimes there was too little text left for too great a space: in such cases, if the manuscript were set as it should have been, a great deal of empty paper would be left free, a condition often described as 'white' space. Sometimes too much text remained for too small a space, and if the manuscript were to be set according to its normal layout, every available inch would be taken up with type (and even then the text might not fit), a condition that could be described as 'crammed space'.

Essentially, this created a huge design problem, and most commentators suggest when it arose the printing house policy was to sacrifice textual accuracy to neatness of design. Thus, so the argument goes, in the case of white space, extra lines of type would have to be created where (presumably) none originally existed. *Hamlet* provides an excellent example with the Polonius speech 'Indeed that's out of the air' starting at line 78 of what most modern texts term Act Two Scene 2. Q2 sets the four-line speech as prose, and most modern texts follow suit. However, F1, faced with a potentially huge white space problem at the bottom of the right hand column of p. 261 in the Tragedy section, resets the speech as eleven lines of very irregular verse! In the case of crammed space, five lines of verse might suddenly become three lines of prose, or in one very severe case of overcrowding in *Henry The Fourth Part Two*, words, phrases, and even half lines of text might be omitted to reduce the text sufficiently.

When such cases occur, this text will set F1 as shown, and the modern texts' suggested alternatives will be footnoted and discussed.

LINE STRUCTURE CHANGES NOT RELATED TO PROBLEMS OF 'CASTING-OFF'

In addition, modern texts regularly make changes to F1's line structure which are not related to 'white' or 'crammed' space, often to the detriment of both character and scene. Two major reasons are offered for the changes.

First, either (a few) prose lines suddenly appear in what essentially is a verse scene (or a few verse lines in a sea of prose) and the modern texts, feeling the scene should be standardised, restructure the offending lines accordingly. *The Tempest* is atrociously served this way[2], for where F1, the only source text, shows the conspirators Caliban, Stephano, and, very occasionally, Trinculo, speaking verse as well as prose even within the same speech (a sure sign of personal striving and inner disturbance) most modern texts readjust the lines to show only Caliban speaking verse (dignifying him more than he deserves) and Stephano and Trinculo only speaking prose (thus robbing them of their dangerous flights of fancy).

Second, some Ff verse lines appear so appallingly defective in terms of their rhythm and length that modern texts feel it necessary to make a few 'readjustments' of the lines around them to bring the offending lines back to a coherent, rhythmic whole. Many of the later plays are abominably served in this regard: in *Macbeth,* for example, over a hundred F1 passages involving more than 200 lines (90 percent of which were set by the usually reliable compositor A) have been altered by most modern texts. Most of these changes concentrate on regularising moments where a character is under tremendous upheaval and hardly likely to be speaking pure formal verse at that particular moment!

These changes come about through a mistaken application of modern grammat-

---

[2] Commentators suggest the copy play used for setting F1, coming from Stratford as it did, and thus unsupervised by Shakespeare in the Playhouse preparation of the document, prepared by Ralph Crane, was at times defective, especially in distinguishing clearly between verse and prose: this is why most modern texts do not follow F1's choices in these dubious passages: readers are invited to explore *The Tempest* within this series, especially the footnotes, as a theatrical vindication of the original F1 setting

ical considerations to texts that were originally prepared not according to grammar but rhetoric. One of rhetoric's many strengths is that it can show not only when characters are in self-control but also when they are not. In a rhetorically set passage, the splutters of a person going through an emotional breakdown, as with Othello, can be shown almost verbatim, with peculiar punctuations, spellings, breaks, and all. If the same passage were to be set grammatically it would be very difficult to show the same degree of personal disintegration on the printed page.[3] F1's occasional weird shifts between verse and prose and back again, together with the moments of extreme linear breakdown, are the equivalents of human emotional breakdown, and once the anomalies of Elizabethan script preparation are accounted for,[4] the rhetorical breakdowns on F1's printed page are clear indications of a character's disintegration within the play. When modern texts tidy up such blemishes grammatically they unwittingly remove essential theatrical and/or character clues for reader and theatre person alike.

In these texts, F1's line structure will be set as is, and all such modern alterations (prose to verse, verse to prose, regularisation of originally unmetrical lines) will be shown. The small symbol ° will be added to show where modern texts suggest a line should end rather than where F1 shows it does. A thin vertical line will be set to the left alongside any text where the modern texts have converted F1's prose to verse, or vice versa. The more large-scale of these changes will be boxed for quicker reader recognition. Most of these changes will be footnoted in the text where they occur, and a comparison of the two different versions of the text and what each could signify theatrically will be offered. For examples of both, see p. xxiii below.

THE SPECIAL PROBLEMS AFFECTING WHAT ARE KNOWN AS 'SHARED' OR 'SPLIT' VERSE LINES

A definition, and their importance to the Shakespeare texts

Essentially, split lines are short lines of verse which, when placed together, form the equivalent of a full verse line. Most commentators suggest they are very useful in speeding the play along, for the second character (whose line attaches on to the end of the first short line) is expected to use the end of the first character's line as a

---

[3] For a full discussion of this, readers are directed to Neil Freeman, *Shakespeare's First Texts* (Vancouver: Folio Scripts, 1994).

[4] Readers are referred to an excellent chapter by Gary Taylor which analyses the whole background, conjectured and known, concerning the preparation of the first scripts. He points out the pitfalls of assuming the early texts as sole authority for all things Shakespearean: he examines the conjectured movement of the scripts from Shakespeare's pen to printed edition, and carefully examples the changes and alterations that could occur, (most notably at the hands of the manuscript copyists), as well as the interferences and revampings of the Playhouse, plus the effects of the first typesetters' personal habits and carelessness. Stanley Wells and Gary Taylor, *William Shakespeare: A Textual Companion* (Oxford: Clarendon Press, 1987), 1–68.

springboard and jump in with an immediate reply, enhancing the quickness of the debate. Thus in *Measure for Measure*, Act Two Scene 2, modern ll. 8–10, the Provost, trying to delay Claudio's execution, has asked Angelo whether Claudio has to die the following day: Angelo's questioning affirmation ends with a very pointed short line, followed immediately by a short line opening from the Provost.

Angelo	Did I not tell thee yea? hadst thou not order?
	Why do'st thou aske againe?
Provost	Lest I might be too rash:
	Under your good correction, I have seene
	When after execution . . .

If the Provost replies immediately after, or just as, Angelo finishes, an explosive dramatic tension is created. Allowing a minor delay before reply, as many actors do, will reduce the impact of the moment, and create a hesitation where one probably does not exist.

The occasional problem

So far so good. But the problems start when more than two short lines follow each other. If there are three short lines in succession, which should be joined, #1 and #2, or #2 and #3? Later in the same scene, Claudio's sister Isabella has, at the insistence of Claudio's friend Lucio, come to plead with Angelo for her brother's life. In Lucio's eyes she is giving up too easily, hence the following (modern ll. 45–49):

Lucio	You are too cold: if you should need a pin,
	You could not with more tame a tongue desire it:
	To him, I say.
Isabella	Must he needs die?
Angelo	Maiden, no remedie?

And here it seems fairly obvious Isabella and Angelo's lines should join together, thus allowing a wonderful dramatic pause following Lucio's urging before Isabella plucks up enough courage to try. Most modern texts set the lines accordingly, with Lucio's the short odd line out.

But what about the three lines contained in the exchange that follows almost straightaway?

Isabella	But you might doe't & do the world no wrong
	If so your heart were touch'd with that remorse,
	As mine is to him?
Angelo	Hee's sentenc'd, tis too late.
Lucio	You are too cold.
Isabella	Too late? why no: I that doe speak a word

> May call it againe: well, beleeve this
> (modern line numbering 53–56)

Does Angelo's 'Hee's sentenc'd...' spring off Isabella's line, leaving Isabella speechless and turning to go before Lucio urges her on again? Or does Angelo pause (to frame a reply?) before speaking, leaving Lucio to quickly jump in quietly giving Isabella no time to back off? Either choice is possible, and dramatically valid. And readers should be allowed to make their own choice, which automatically means each reader should able to see the possibility of such choices when they occur.

The problem magnified by the way modern texts set split/shared lines

However, because of a peculiarity faced by the modern texts not shared by Ff/Qq, modern texts rarely show such possibilities to their readers but make the choice for them. The peculiarity comes about from a change in text layout initiated in the eighteenth century.

Ff/Qq always set short lines directly under one another, as shown in the examples above. In 1778 George Steevens, a highly respected editor, started to show split lines a new way, by advancing the second split line to just beyond where the first split line finishes, viz.

> Angelo   Did I not tell thee yea? hadst thou not order?
>   Why do'st thou aske againe?
>
> Provost   Lest I might be too rash:
>   Under your good correction, I have seene
>   When after execution...

Since that date all editions of Shakespeare have followed this practice, which is fine as long as there are only two short lines, but when three follow each other, a choice has to be made. Thus the second Isabella/Angelo/Lucio sequence could be set as either

> Isabella   But you might doe't & do the world no wrong
>   If so your heart were touch'd with that remorse,
>   As mine is to him?
>
> Angelo   Hee's sentenc'd, tis too late.
>
> Lucio   You are too cold.
>
> Isabella   Too late? why no: I that doe speak a word
>   May call it againe: well, beleeve this...

(the usual modern choice), or

> Isabella   But you might doe't & do the world no wrong
>   If so your heart were touch'd with that remorse,
>   As mine is to him?

Angelo	Hee's sentenc'd, tis too late.
Lucio	You are too cold.
Isabella	Too late? why no: I that doe speak a word May call it againe: well, beleeve this ...

This modern typesetting convention has robbed the reader of a very important moment of choice. Indeed, at the beginning of the twentieth century, Richard Flatter[5] suggested that what modern commentators consider to be split lines may not be split lines at all. He offers two other suggestions: pauses and hesitations could exist between each line, or the lines could in fact be spoken one on top of another, a very important consideration for the crowd responses to Anthony in the funeral scene of *Julius Caesar.* Either way, the universally adopted Steevens layout precludes the reader/theatre practitioner from even seeing such possibilities.

These texts will show the F1 layout as is, and will indicate via footnote when a choice is possible (in the case of three short lines, or more, in succession) and by the symbol } when the possibility of springboarding exists. Thus the Folio Texts would show the first Angelo/Provost example as:

Angelo	Did I not tell thee yea? hadst thou not order? Why do'st thou aske againe? }
Provost	Lest I might be too rash: Under your good correction, I have seene When after execution ...

In nearly all cases the } shows where most modern texts insist on setting a shared split line. However, readers are cautioned that in many of the later plays, the single line so created is much longer than pentameter, and often very a-rhythmic. In such cases the lines could have great value as originally set (two separate short lines), especially when a key debate is in process (for example, *Measure for Measure, The Tragedie of Cymbeline, Othello,* and *The Winters Tale*).

THE UNUSUAL SINGLE SPLIT LINE (PLEASE SEE 'A CAVEAT', P. XXXVIII)

So far the discussion has centred on short lines shared by two or more characters. Ff/Qq offer another complication rarely, if ever, accepted by most modern texts. Quite often, and not because of white space, a single character will be given two consecutive short lines within a single speech. *Romeo and Juliet* is chock full of this device: in the famous balcony scene (modern texts numbering 2.2.62–3) Juliet asks Romeo

How cam'st thou hither.

---

[5]   Richard Flatter, *Shakespeare's Producing Hand* (London: Heinemann, 1948, reprint).

>Tell me, and wherefore?
>The Orchard walls are high, and hard to climbe

The first two lines (five syllables each) suggest a minute pause between them as Juliet hesitates before asking the all important second line (with its key second part 'and wherefore'). Since Qq rarely set such 'single split lines' most modern texts refuse to set any of them, but combine them:

>How cams't thou hither. Tell me and wherefore?

This basically F1 device is set by all the compositors and followed by all other Folios. This text will follow suit, highlighting them with the symbol → for quick recognition, viz.:

>How cam'st thou hither. →
>Tell me, and wherefore?
>The Orchard walls are high, and hard to climbe

SENTENCE AND PUNCTUATION STRUCTURES

A CHARACTER'S THOUGHTFUL & EMOTIONAL JOURNEY

A quick comparison between these texts and both the Ff/Qq's and the modern texts will reveal two key differences in the layout of the dialogue on the printed page — the bolding of major punctuation, and the single line dropping of text whenever a new sentence begins.

The underlying principle behind these texts is that since the handwritten documents from which they stem were originally intended for the actor and Playhouse, in addition to their poetical values, the Ff/Qq scripts represent a theatrical process. Even if the scripts are being read just for pleasure, at the back of the reader's mind should be the notion of characters on a stage and actors acting (and the word 'process' rather than 'practice' is deliberate, with process suggesting a progression, development, or journey).

The late Jean-Louis Barrault gave a wonderful definition of acting, and of this journey, suggesting an actor's job was to strive to remain in 'the ever-changing present'. If something happens onstage (an entry, an exit, a verbal acceptance or denial of what the actor's character has suggested), the 'present' has changed, and the character must readjust accordingly. Just as onstage, the actor should be prepared for the character to re-adjust, and in rehearsal should be examining how and why it does, so should the reader in the library, armchair, or classroom.

In many ways, the key to Shakespeare is discovering how each character's mind works; perceiving the emotions and intellects as they act and react helps the reader understand from where the poetical imagination and utterance stem.

Certain elements of each character's emotional and intellectual journey, and where it changes, are encoded into the sentence structure of Ff/Qq.

Elizabethan education prepared any schooled individual (via the 'petty school' and the private tutor) for the all important and essential daily rough and tumble of argument and debate. Children were trained not only how to frame an argument so as to win it hands down, but also how to make it entertaining so as to enthrall the neutral listener.

The overall training, known as 'rhetoric', essentially allowed intellect and emotion to exist side by side, encouraging the intellect to keep the emotion in check. The idea was not to deny the emotions, but ensure they didn't swamp the 'divinity' of reason, the only thing separating man from beast. While the initial training was mainly vocal, any written matter of the period automatically reflected the ebb and flow of debate. What was set on the printed page was not grammar, but a representation of the rhetorical process.

DROPPING A LINE TO ILLUSTRATE F1'S SENTENCE STRUCTURE

Put at its simplest, in any document of the period, each sentence would represent a new intellectual and emotional stage of a rhetorical argument. When this stage of the argument was completed, a period would be set (occasionally a question mark or, much more rarely, an exclamation mark—both followed by a capital letter) signifying the end of that stage of the argument, and the beginning of the next.

Thus in the First Folio, the identification of each new sentence is an automatic (and for us, four hundred years later, a wonderful) aid to understanding how a character is reacting to and dealing with Barrault's ever-changing present.

To help the reader quickly spot the new steppingstone in an argument, and thus the point of transition, these texts highlight where one sentence ends and the new one begins by simply dropping a line whenever a new sentence starts. Thus the reader has a visual reminder that the character is making a transition to deal with a change in the current circumstances of the scene (or in the process of self-discovery in the case of soliloquies).

This device has several advantages. The reader can instantly see where the next step in the argument begins. The patterns so created on the page can quickly illuminate whenever a contrast between characters' thought patterns occurs. (Sometimes the sentences are short and precise, suggesting the character is moving quickly from one idea to the next. Sometimes the sentences are very long, suggesting the character is undergoing a very convoluted process. Sometimes the sentences contain nothing but facts, suggesting the character has no time to entertain; sometimes they are filled with high-flown imagery, perhaps suggesting the character is trying to mask a very weak argument with verbal flummery.) The patterns can also show when a character's style changes within itself, say from long and convoluted to short and precise, or vice versa. It can also immediately pinpoint when a character is in trouble and not arguing coherently or logically, something modern texts often alter out of grammatical necessity.

With patience, all this could be gleaned from the modern texts (in as far as they set the Ff sentence structure, which they often don't) and from a photostat of the First Folio, by paying special attention to where the periods are set. But there is one extra very special advantage to this new device of dropping a line: this has to do once more with the Elizabethan method of setting down spoken argument on paper, especially when the character speaking is not in the best of all possible worlds.

If an Elizabethan person/character is arguing well, neatly, cleanly, tidily, then a printed representation of that argument would also be clean, neat, and tidy—to modern eyes it would be grammatically acceptable. If the same character is emotionally upset, or incapable of making a clear and tidy argument, then the on-paper representation would be muddy and untidy—to modern eyes totally ungrammatical and often not acceptable. By slightly isolating each sentence these texts very quickly allow the reader to spot when a sentence's construction is not all that it should be, say in the middle of Viola's so-called ring speech in *Twelfth Night* (Act Two Scene 2), or Helena's declaration of love for Bertram in *All's Well That Ends Well* (Act One Scene 3), or the amazing opening to *As You Like It,* where Orlando's opening litany of complaint against his brother starts with a single sentence twenty lines long.

This is especially relevant when a surprising modern editorial practice is accounted for. Very often the Ff sentence structures are markedly altered by modern texts, especially when the Ff sentences do not seem 'grammatical'—thus Orlando's twenty-line monster is split into six separate, grammatically correct sentences by all modern texts. And then there is the case of Shylock in *The Merchant of Venice,* a Jewish man being goaded and tormented beyond belief by the very Christians who helped his daughter elope with a Christian, taking a large part of Shylock's fortune with her. A sentence comparison of the famous Act Three Scene 1 speech culminating in 'Hath not a Jew eyes?' is very instructive. All modern texts set the speech as between fifteen and seventeen sentences in length: whatever the pain, anger, and personal passion, the modern texts encourage dignity and self-control, a rational Shylock. But this is a Shylock completely foreign to both Q1 and Ff. Q1 show the same speech as only four sentences long, Ff five—a veritable onflow of intellect and passion all mixed together, all unstoppable for the longest period of time—a totally different being from that shown by the modern texts. What is more, this is a totally different Shylock from the one seen earlier in the Ff/Q1 version of the play, where, even in the extremes of discomfort with the old enemy Anthonio, his sentence structures are rhetorically balanced and still grammatical to modern eyes.

Here, with Shylock, there are at least three benefits to dropping the sentence: the unusualness of the speech is immediately spotted; the change in style between this and any of his previous speeches can be quickly seen; and, above all, the moment where the speech moves from a long unchecked outpouring to a quick series of brief, dangerously rational sentences can be quickly identified. And these advantages will be seen in such changed sentence circumstances in any play in any of these texts.

THE HIGHLIGHTING OF THE MAJOR PUNCTUATION IN THESE TEXTS

A second key element of rhetoric encoded into the Ff/Qq texts clearly shows the characters' mind in action. The encoding lies in the remaining punctuation which, unlike much modern punctuation, serves a double function, one dealing with the formation of the thought, the other with the speaking of it.

Apart from the period, dealt with already, essentially there are two sets of punctuation to consider, minor and major, each with their own very specific functions.

Shakespearean characters reflect the mode of thinking of their time. Elizabethans were trained to constantly add to or modify thoughts. They added a thought to expand the one already made. They denied the first thought so as to set up alternatives. They elaborated a thought so as to clarify what has already been said. They suddenly moved into splendid puns or non-sequiturs (emotional, logical, or both) because they had been immediately stimulated by what they or others had just said. The **minor punctuation** (essentially the comma [,] the parenthesis or bracket [( )], and the dash) reflects all this.

In establishing thought processes for each character, minor punctuation shows every new nuance of thought: every tiny punctuation in this category helps establish the deftness and dance of each character's mind. In *As You Like It* (Act Three Scene 2, modern line numbering 400–402) the Ff setting of Rosalind's playing with her beloved Orlando has a wonderful coltish exuberance as she runs rings round his protestations of love:

> Love is meerely a madnesse, and I tel you,
> deserves as well a darke house,* and a whip,* as madmen do:

Her mind is adding extra thoughts as she goes: the Ff commas are as much part of her spirit and character as the words are—though most modern texts create a much more direct essayist, preaching what she already knows, by removing the two Ff commas marked *.[6]

A similar situation exists with Macbeth, facing Duncan whom he must kill if he is

---

[6] Unfortunately, many modern texts eradicate the F and Q minor punctuation arguing the need for light (or infrequent) punctuation to preserve the speed of speech. This is not necessarily helpful, since what it removes is just a new thought marker, not an automatic indication to pause: too often the result is that what the first texts offer a character as a series of closely-worked out dancing thought-patterns (building one quick thought—as marked by a comma—on top of another) is turned into a series of much longer phrases: often, involved and reactive busy minds are artificially turned into (at best) eloquent ones, suddenly capable of perfect and lengthy rationality where the situation does not warrant such a reaction, or (at worst) vapid ones, speaking an almost preconceived essay of commentary or artificial sentimentality.

to become king (Act One Scene 4, modern line numbering 22–27). Ff show a Macbeth almost swamped with extra thoughts as he assures Duncan

> The service,* and the loyaltie I owe,
> In doing it,* payes it selfe.
> Your highnesse part,* is to receive our Duties,
> And our Duties are to your Throne,* and State,
> Children,* and Servants; which doe but what they should,*
> By doing every thing safe toward your Love
> And Honour.

The heavy use of minor punctuation—especially when compared with most modern texts which remove the commas marked *, leaving Macbeth with just six thoughts compared to Ff's twelve—clearly shows a man ill at ease and/or working too hard to say the right thing. Again the punctuation helps create an understanding of the character.

However, while the minor punctuation is extremely important in the discovery process of reading and/or rehearsal, paradoxically, it mustn't become too dominant. From the performance/speaking viewpoint, to pause at each comma would be tantamount to disaster. There would be an enormous dampening effect if reader/actor were to pause at every single piece of punctuation: the poetry would be destroyed and the event would become interminable.

In many ways, minor punctuation is the Victorian child of Shakespearean texts, it must be seen but not heard. (In speaking the text, the new thought the minor punctuation represents can be added without pausing: a change in timbre, rhythm, or pitch—in acting terms, occurring naturally with changes in intention—will do the trick.)

But once thoughts have been discovered, they have to be organised into some form of coherent whole. If the period shows the end of one world and the start of the new, and if the comma marks a series of small, ever-changing, ever-evolving thoughts within each world, occasionally there must be pause for reflection somewhere in the helter-skelter of tumbling new ideas. This is the **major punctuation's** strength; major punctuation consisting of the semicolon [;], and the colon [:].

Major punctuation marks the gathering together of a series of small thoughts within an overall idea before moving onto something new. If a room full of Rodin sculptures were analogous to an Elizabethan scene or act, each individual piece of sculpture would be a speech, the torso or back or each major limb a separate sentence. Each collective body part (a hand, the wrist, the forearm, the upper arm) would be a series of small thoughts bounded by major punctuation, each smaller item within that part (a finger, a fingernail, a knuckle) a single small thought separated by commas. In describing the sculpture to a friend one might move from the smaller details (the knuckle) to the larger (the hand) to another larger (the wrist) then another (the forearm) and so on to the whole limb. Unless the speaker is emotionally moved by the recollection, some pauses would be essential, certainly after finishing the whole description of the arm (the sentence), and probably after each major collective of the hand, the wrist, etc. (as marked by the major punctuation), but not after every small bit.

As a rule of thumb, and simply stated, the colon and semicolon mark both a thinking and a speaking pause. The vital difference between major and minor punctuation, whether in the silent reading of the text or the performing of it aloud, is you need not pause at the comma, bracket, or dash; you probably should at the colon, semicolon, and period.

Why the Major Punctuation is Bolded in These Texts.

In speaking the text or reading it, the minor punctuation indicates the need to key onto the new thought without necessarily requiring a pause. In so doing, the inherent rhythms of speech, scene, and play can clip along at the rate suggested by the Prologue in *Romeo and Juliet,* 'the two hours traffic of the stage', until a pause is absolutely necessary. Leave the commas alone, and the necessary pauses will make themselves known.

The 'major' punctuation then comes into its own, demanding double attention as both a thinking and speaking device. This is why it is bolded, to highlight it for the reader's easier access. The reader can still use all the punctuation when desired, working through the speech thought by thought, taking into account both major and minor punctuation as normal. Then, when needed, the bolding of the major punctuation will allow the reader easy access for marking where the speech, scene, or play needs to be broken down into its larger thinking/speaking (and even breathing) units without affecting its overall flow.

The Blank Pages Within the Text

In each text within this series, once readers reach the play itself they will find that with each pair of pages the dialogue is printed on the right-hand page only. The left-hand page has been deliberately left blank so that readers, actors, directors, stage managers, teachers, etc. have ample space for whatever notes and text emendations they may wish to add.

PRACTICAL ON-PAGE HELP FOR THE READER

THE VISUAL SYMBOLS HIGHLIGHTING MODERN ALTERATIONS

THE BOX

This surrounds a passage where the modern texts have made whole-scale alterations to the Ff text. Each boxed section will be footnoted, and the changes analysed at the bottom of the page.

THE FOOTNOTES

With many modern texts the footnotes are not easily accessible. Often no indication is given within the text itself where the problem/choice/correction exists. Readers are forced into a rather cumbersome four-step process. First, they have to search through the bottom of the page where the footnotes are crammed together, often in very small print, to find a line number where an alteration has been made. Then they must read the note to find out what has been altered. Then they must go back to the text and search the side of the page to find the corresponding line number. Having done all this, finally they can search the line to find the word or phrase that has been changed (sometimes complicated by the fact the word in question is set twice in different parts of the line).

These texts will provide a reference marker within the text itself, directly alongside the word or phrase that is in question. This guides the reader directly to the corresponding number in the footnote section of the bottom of each page, to the alteration under discussion — hopefully a much quicker and more immediate process.

In addition, since there are anywhere between 300 and 1,100 footnotes in any one of these texts, a tool is offered to help the reader find only those notes they require, when they require them. In the footnote section, prior to the number that matches the footnote marker in the text, a letter or combination of letters will be set as a code. The letter 'W', for example, shows that the accompanying footnote refers to word substitutions offered by modern texts; the letters 'SD' refer to an added or altered stage direction; the letters 'LS' show the footnote deals with a passage where the modern texts have completely altered the line-structure that F1 set. This enables readers to be selective when they want to examine only certain changes, for they can quickly skim through the body of footnotes until they find the code they want, perhaps those dealing with changes in prefixes (the code 'P') or when modern alterations have been swapping lines from verse to prose or vice versa (the code 'VP') For full details of the codes, see pp. xxxiii–xxxv below.

Readers are urged to make full use of the footnotes in any of the Recommended Texts listed just before the start of the play. They are excellent in their areas of expertise. To attempt to rival or paraphrase them would be redundant. Thus the footnotes in these scripts will hardly ever deal with word meanings and derivations; social or political history; literary derivations and comparisons; or lengthy quotations from scholars or commentators. Such information is readily available in the *Oxford English Dictionary* and from the recommended modern texts.

Generally, the footnotes in these scripts will deal with matters theatrical and textual and will be confined to three major areas: noting where and how the modern texts alter F1's line structure; showing popular alternative word readings often selected by the modern texts (these scripts will keep the F1 reading unless otherwise noted); and showing the rare occasions where and how these scripts deviate from their source texts. When the modern texts offer alternative words and/or phrases to F2-4/Qq, the original spelling and punctuation will be used. Where appropriate, the footnotes will briefly refer to the excellent research of the scholars of the last three centuries, and to possible theatrical reasons for maintaining F1's structural 'irregularities'.

THE SYMBOL °

This will be used to show where modern texts have altered F1's line structure, and will allow the reader to explore both the F1 setting and the modern alternative while examining the speech where it is set, in its proper context and rightful position within the play. For example, though F1 is usually the source text for *Henry the Fifth* and sets the dialogue for Pistoll in prose, most modern texts use the memorial Q version and change his lines to (at times extraordinarily peculiar) verse. These texts will set the speech as shown in F1, but add the ° to show the modern texts alterations, thus:

> Pistoll Fortune is Bardolphs foe, and frownes on him:°
> for he hath stolne a Pax, and hanged must a be:° a damned
> death:° let Gallowes gape for Dogge, let Man goe free,°
> and let not Hempe his Wind-pipe suffocate:° but Exeter
> hath given the doome of death,° for Pax of little price.°
>
> Therefore goe speake,° the Duke will heare thy voyce;°
> and let not Bardolphs vitall thred bee cut° with edge of
> Penny-Cord, and vile reproach.°
>   Speake Captaine for
> his Life, and I will thee requite.°
>   (*Henry V*, These Scripts, 2.1.450–459)

Read the speech utilising the ° to mark the end of a line, and the reader is exploring what the modern texts suggest should be the structure. Read the lines ignoring the ° and the reader is exploring what the F1 text really is. Thus both F1 and modern/Q versions can be read within the body of the text.

THE VERTICAL LINE TO THE LEFT OF THE TEXT

This will be used to mark a passage where modern editors have altered F1's verse to prose or vice versa. Here is a passage in a predominantly prose scene from *Henry V.* Modern texts and F1 agree that Williams and Fluellen should be set in prose. However, the F1 setting for Henry could be in verse, though most modern texts set it in prose too. The thin vertical line to the left of the text is a quick reminder to the reader of disagreement between Ff and modern texts (the F1 setting will always be shown, and the disputed section will be footnoted accordingly).

> King Henry Twas I indeed thou promised'st to strike,
> And thou hast given me most bitter termes.
>
> Fluellen And please your Majestie, let his Neck answere
> for it, if there is any Marshall Law in the World.
>
> King Henry How canst thou make me satisfaction?
>
> Williams All offences, my Lord, come from the heart: ne-
> ver came any from mine, that might offend your Ma-
> jestie. (*Henry V,* These Scripts, 4.1.240–247)

THE SYMBOL } SET TO THE RIGHT OF TEXT, CONNECTING TWO SPEECHES

This will be used to remind readers of the presence of what most modern texts consider to be split or shared lines, and that therefore the second speech could springboard quickly off the first, thus increasing the speed of the dialogue and debate; for example:

> Angelo Did I not tell thee yea? hadst thou not order?
> Why do'st thou aske againe?
> }
> Provost Lest I might be too rash:
> Under your good correction, I have seene
> When after execution . . .

Since there is no definitive way of determining whether Shakespeare wished the two short lines to be used as a shared or split line, or used as two separate short lines, the reader would do well to explore the moment twice. The first time the second speech could be 'springboarded' off the first as if it were a definite shared line; the second time round a tiny break could be inserted before speaking the second speech, as if a hesitation were deliberately intended. This way both possibilities of the text can be examined.

THE SYMBOL → TO THE RIGHT OF THE TEXT, JOINING TWO SHORT LINES SPOKEN BY A SINGLE CHARACTER

This indicates that though Ff has set two short lines for a single character, perhaps hinting at a minute break between the two thoughts, most modern texts have set the two short lines as one longer one. Thus the first two lines of Juliet's

> How cam'st thou hither. →

> Tell me, and wherefore?
> The Orchard walls are high, and hard to climbe

can be explored as one complete line (the interpretation of most modern texts), or, as F1 suggests, as two separate thoughts with a tiny hesitation between them. In most cases these lines will be footnoted, and possible reasons for the F1 interpretation explored.

THE OCCASIONAL USE OF THE †

This marks where F1 has been forced, in a crowded line, to set the end of the line immediately above or below the first line, flush to the right hand column. These texts will set the original as one complete line—the only instance where these scripts do not faithfully reproduce F1's line structure.

THE OCCASIONAL USE OF THE † TOGETHER WITH A FOOTNOTE (ALSO SEE P. XXXVII)

This marks where a presumed F1 compositorial mistake has led to a meaningless word being set (for example 'speeh' instead of 'speech') and, since there is a 'correct' form of the word offered by either F2–4 or Qq, the correct form of the word rather than the F1 error has been set. The footnote directs the reader to the original F1 setting reproduced at the bottom of the page.

PATTERNED BRACKETS { } SURROUNDING A PREFIX OR PART OF A STAGE DIRECTION

These will be used on the infrequent occasions where a minor alteration or addition has been made to the original F1 setting.

THE VARIED USE OF THE * AND ∞

This will change from text to text. Sometimes (as in *Hamlet*) an * will be used to show where, because of the 1606 Acte To Restraine The Abuses of Players, F1 had to alter Qq's 'God' to 'Heaven'. In other plays it may be used to show the substitution of the archaic 'a' for 'he' while in others the * and /or the ∞ may be used to denote a line from Qq or F2–4 which F1 omits.

THE SYMBOL •

This is a reminder that a character with several prefixes has returned to one previously used in the play.

THE VISUAL SYMBOLS HIGHLIGHTING KEY ITEMS WITHIN THE FIRST FOLIO

THE DROPPING OF THE TEXT A SINGLE LINE

This indicates where one sentence ends, and a new one begins (see pp. xvii–xviii).

THE BOLDING OF PUNCTUATION

This indicates the presence of the major punctuation (see pp. xviii–xxi).

UNBRACKETED STAGE DIRECTIONS

These are the ones presumed to come from the manuscript copy closest to Shakespeare's own hand (F1 sets them centred, on a separate line). They usually have a direct effect on the scene, altering what has been taking place immediately prior to its setting (see p. ix).

BRACKETED STAGE DIRECTIONS

These are the ones presumed to have been added by the Playhouse. (F1 sets them alongside the dialogue, flush to the right of the column.) They usually support, rather than alter, the onstage action (see p. ix).

(The visual difference in the two sets of directions can quickly point the reader to an unexpected aspect of an entry or exit. Occasionally an entry is set alongside the text, rather than on a separate line. This might suggest the character enters not wishing to draw attention to itself, for example, towards the end of *Macbeth,* the servant entering with the dreadful news of the moving Byrnane Wood. Again, F1 occasionally sets an exit on a separate line, perhaps stopping the onstage action altogether, as with the triumphal exit to a 'Gossips feast' at the end of *The Comedy of Errors* made by most of the reunited and/or business pacified characters, leaving the servant Dromio twins onstage to finish off the play. A footnote will be added when these unusual variations in F1's directions occur.)

As with all current texts, the final period of any bracketed or unbracketed stage direction will not be set.

ACT, SCENE, AND LINE NUMBERING SPECIFIC TO THIS TEXT

Each of these scripts will show the act and scene division from F1. They will also indicate modern act and scene division, which often differs from Ff/Qq. Modern texts suggest that in many plays full scene division was not attempted until the eighteenth century, and act division in the early texts was sometimes haphazard at best. Thus many modern texts place the act division at a point other than that set in Ff/Qq, and nearly always break Ff/Qq text up into extra scenes. When modern texts add an act or scene division which is not shared by F1, the addition will be shown in brackets within the body of each individual play as it occurs. When Ff set a new Act or scene, for clarity these texts will start a fresh page, even though this is not Ff/Qq practice

ON THE LEFT HAND SIDE OF EACH PAGE

Down the left of each page, line numbers are shown in increments of five. These refer to the lines in this text only. Where F1 prints a line containing two sentences, since these scripts set two separate lines, each line will be numbered independently.

ON THE TOP RIGHT OF EACH PAGE

These numbers represent the first and last lines set on the page, and so summarise the information set down the left hand side of the text.

AT THE BOTTOM RIGHT OF EACH PAGE: USING THESE SCRIPTS WITH OTHER TEXTS

At times a reader may want to compare these texts with either the original First Folio, or a reputable modern text, or both. Specially devised line numbers will make this a fairly easy proposition. These new reference numbers will be found at the bottom right of the page, just above the footnote section.

The information before the colon allows the reader to compare these texts against any photographic reproduction of the First Folio. The information after the colon allows the reader to compare these texts with a modern text, specifically the excellent *Riverside Shakespeare.*[7]

Before the colon: any photostat of the First Folio

A capital letter plus a set of numbers will be shown followed by a lowercase letter. The numbers refer the reader to a particular page within the First Folio; the capital letter before the numbers specifies whether the reader should be looking at the right hand column (R) or left hand column (L) on that particular page; the lower case letter after the numbers indicates which compositor (mainly 'a' through 'e') set that particular column. An occasional asterisk alongside the reference tells the reader that though this is the page number as set in F1, it is in fact numbered out of sequence, and care is needed to ensure, say in *Cymbeline,* the appropriate one of two 'p. 389s' is being consulted.

Since the First Folio was printed in three separate sections (the first containing the Comedies, the second the Histories, and the third the Tragedies),[8] the pages and section in which each of these scripts is to be found will be mentioned in the introduction accompanying each play. The page number refers to that printed at the top of the reproduced Folio page, and not to the number that appears at the bottom of the page of the book which contains the reproduction.

Thus, from this series of texts, page one of *Measure for Measure* shows the ref-

---

[7]   Gwynne Blakemore Evans, Harry Levin, Anne Barton, Herschel Baker, Frank Kermode, Hallet D. Smith, and Marie Edel, eds., *The Riverside Shakespeare* (Copyright © 1974 by Houghton Mifflin Company). This work is chosen for its exemplary scholarship, editing principles, and footnotes.

[8]   The plays known as Romances were not printed as a separate section: *Cymbeline* was set with the Tragedies, *The Winter's Tale* and *The Tempest* were set within the Comedies, and though *Pericles* had been set in Q it did not appear in the compendium until F3. *Troilus and Cressida* was not assigned to any section, but was inserted between the Histories and the Tragedies with only 2 of its 28 pages numbered.

erence 'L61–c'. This tells the reader that the text was set by compositor 'c' and can be checked against the left hand column of p. 61 of the First Folio (*Measure For Measure* being set in the Comedy Section of F1).

Occasionally the first part of the reference seen at the bottom of the page will also be seen within the text, somewhere on the right hand side of the page. This shows the reader exactly where this column has ended and the new one begins.

(As any photostat of the First Folio clearly shows, there are often sixty-five lines or more per column, sometimes crowded very close together. The late Professor Charlton Hinman employed a brilliantly simple line-numbering system (known as TLN, short for Through Line Numbering System) whereby readers could quickly be directed to any particular line within any column on any page.

The current holders of the rights to the TLN withheld permission for the system to be used in conjunction with this series of Folio Texts.)

After the colon: *The Riverside Shakespeare*

Numbers will be printed indicating the act, scene, and line numbers in *The Riverside Shakespeare,* which contain the information set on the particular page of this script. Again, using the first page of *Measure For Measure*, the reference 1.1.1–21 on page one of these scripts directs the reader to Act One Scene 1 of *The Riverside Shakespeare*; line one in *The Riverside Shakespeare* matches the first line in this text, while the last line of dialogue on page one of this text is to be found in line twenty-one of the *Riverside* version of the play.

COMMON TYPESETTING PECULIARITIES
OF THE FOLIO AND QUARTO TEXTS
(And How These Texts Present Them)

There are a few (to modern eyes) unusual contemporary Elizabethan and early Jacobean printing practices which will be retained in these scripts.

THE ABBREVIATIONS, 'S.', 'L.', 'D.', 'M.'

Ff and Qq use standard printing abbreviations when there is not enough space on a single line to fit in all the words. The most recognisable to modern eyes includes 'S.' for Saint; 'L.' for Lord; 'M.' for Mister (though this can also be short for 'Master', 'Monsieur', and on occasions even 'Mistress'); and 'D.' for Duke. These scripts will set F1 and footnote accordingly.

'Ÿ', 'W', AND ACCENTED FINAL VOWELS

Ff/Qq's two most commonly used abbreviations are not current today, viz.:
　　ÿ, which is usually shorthand for either 'you'; 'thee'; 'thou'; 'thy'; 'thine'; or 'yours'
　　w, usually with a ¨ above, shorthand for either 'which'; 'what'; 'when'; or 'where'.
Also, in other cases of line overcrowding, the last letter of a relatively unimportant word is omitted, and an accent placed over the preceding vowel as a marker, e.g. 'thä' for 'than'. For all such abbreviations these scripts will set F1 and footnote accordingly.

THE SPECIAL CASE OF THE QUESTION AND EXCLAMATION MARKS ('?' AND '!')

Usage

Elizabethan use of these marks differs somewhat from modern practice. Ff/Qq rarely set an exclamation mark: instead the question mark was used either both as a question mark and as an exclamation point. Thus occasionally the question mark suggests some minor emphasis in the reading.

Sentence Count

When either mark occurs in the middle of a speech, it can be followed by a capitalised or a lowercase word. When the word is lowercase (not capitalised) the sentence continues on without a break. The opposite is not always true: just because the following word is capitalised does not automatically signify the start of a new sentence, though more often than not it does.

Elizabethan rhetorical writing style allowed for words to be capitalised within a sentence, a practice continued by the F1 compositors. Several times in *The Winters Tale,* highly emotional speeches are set full of question marks followed by capitalised words. Each speech could be either one long sentence of ongoing passionate rush, or up to seven shorter sentences attempting to establish self-control.

The final choice belongs to the individual reader, and in cases where such alternatives arise, the passages will be boxed, footnoted, and the various possibilities discussed.

THE ENDING OF SPEECHES WITH NO PUNCTUATION, OR PUNCTUATION OTHER THAN A PERIOD

Quite often F1–2 will not show punctuation at the end of a speech, or sometimes set a colon (:) or a comma (,) instead. Some commentators suggest the setting of anything other than a period was due to compositor carelessness, and that omission occurred either for the same reason, or because the text was so full it came flush to the right hand side of the column and there was no room left for the final punctuation to be set. Thus modern texts nearly always end a speech with the standard period (.), question mark (?), or exclamation mark (!), no matter what F1–2 have set.

However, omission doesn't always occur when a line is full, and F2, though making over sixteen hundred unauthorised typographical corrections of F1 (more than eight hundred of which are accepted by most modern texts), rarely replaces an offending comma or colon with a period, or adds missing periods — F3 is the first to make such alterations on a large scale basis. A few commentators, while acknowledging some of the omissions/mistakes are likely to be due to compositor or scribal error, suggest that ending the speech with anything other than a period (or not ending the speech at all) might indicate that the character with the speech immediately following is in fact interrupting this first speaker.

These texts will set F1, footnote accordingly, and sometimes discuss the possible effect of the missing or 'incorrect' punctuation.

THE SUBSTITUTIONS OF 'i/I' FOR 'j/J' AND 'u' FOR 'v'

In both Ff/Qq words now spelled as 'Jove' or 'Joan' are often set as 'Iove' or 'Ioan'. To avoid confusion, these texts will set the modern version of the word. Similarly, words with 'v' in the middle are often set by Ff/Qq with a 'u'; thus the modern word 'avoid' becomes 'auoid'. Again, these texts will set the modern version of the word, without footnote acknowledgement.

ALTERNATIVE SETTINGS OF A WORD WHERE DIFFERENT SPELLINGS MAINTAIN THE SAME MEANING

Ff/Qq occasionally set, what appears to modern eyes, an archaic spelling of a word for which there is a more common modern alternative, for example 'murther' for murder, 'burthen' for burden, 'moe' for more, 'vilde' for vile. Some modern texts set the Ff/Qq spelling, some modernise. These texts will set the F1 spelling throughout.

ALTERNATIVE SETTINGS OF A WORD WHERE DIFFERENT SPELLINGS SUGGEST DIFFERENT MEANINGS

Far more complicated is the situation where, while an Elizabethan could substitute one word formation for another and still imply the same thing, to modern eyes the substituted word has a entirely different meaning to the one it has replaced. The following is by no means an exclusive list of the more common dual-spelling, dual-meaning words:

anticke–antique	mad–made	sprite–spirit
born–borne	metal–mettle	sun–sonne
hart–heart	mote–moth	travel–travaill
human–humane	pour–(powre)–power	through–thorough
lest–least	reverent–reverend	troth–truth
lose–loose	right–rite	whether–whither

Some of these doubles offer a metrical problem too; for example 'sprite', a one syllable word, versus 'spirit'. A potential problem occurs in *A Midsummer Nights Dream*, where provided the modern texts set Q1's 'thorough', the scansion pattern of elegant magic can be established, whereas F1's more plebeian 'through' sets up a much more awkward and clumsy moment.

These texts will set the F1 reading, and footnote where the modern texts' substitution of a different word formation has the potential to alter the meaning (and sometimes scansion) of the line.

'THEN' AND 'THAN'

These two words, though their neutral vowels sound different to modern ears, were almost identical to Elizabethan speakers and readers, despite their different meanings. Ff and Qq make little distinction between them, setting them interchangeably. In these scripts the original printings will be used, and the modern reader should soon get used to substituting one for the other as necessary.

'I', AND 'AY'

Ff/Qq often print the personal pronoun 'I' and the word of agreement 'aye' simply as 'I'. Again, the modern reader should quickly get used to this and make the substitution whenever necessary. The reader should also be aware that very occasionally either word could be used and the phrase make perfect sense, even though different meanings would be implied.

'MY SELFE/HIM SELFE/HER SELFE' VERSUS 'MYSELF /HIMSELF / HERSELF'

Generally Ff/Qq separate the two parts of the word, 'my selfe' while most modern texts set the single word 'myself'. The difference is vital, based on Elizabethan philosophy. Elizabethans regarded themselves as composed of two parts, the corporeal 'I', and the more spiritual part, the 'selfe'. Thus when an Elizabethan character refers to 'my selfe', he or she is often referring to what is to all intents and purposes a separate being, even if that being is a particular part of him- or herself. Thus soliloquies can be thought of as a debate between the 'I' and 'my selfe', and in such speeches, even though there may be only one character onstage, it's as if there were two distinct entities present.

These texts will show F1 as set.

FOOTNOTE CODE
(shown in two forms, the first alphabetical, the second grouping the codes by topic)

To help the reader focus on a particular topic or research aspect, a special code has been developed for these texts. Each footnote within the footnote section at the bottom of each page of text has a single letter or series of letters placed in front of it guiding readers to one specific topic; thus 'SPD' will direct readers to footnotes just dealing with songs, poems, and doggerel.

ALPHABETICAL FOOTNOTE CODING

A	asides
AB	abbreviation
ADD	a passage modern texts have added to their texts from F2–4/Qq
ALT	a passage (including act and scene division) that has been altered by modern texts without any Ff/Qq authority
COMP	a setting probably influenced by compositor interference
F	concerning disputed facts within the play
FL	foreign language
L	letter or letters
LS	alterations in line structure
M	Shakespeare's use of the scansion of magic (trochaic and seven syllables)
N	a name modern texts have changed or corrected for easier recognition
O	F1 words or phrases substituted for a Qq oath or blasphemy
OM	passage, line, or word modern texts omit or suggest omitting
P	change in prefix assigned to a character
PCT	alterations to F1's punctuation by modern and/or contemporary texts
Q	material rejected or markedly altered by Qq not usually set by modern texts
QO	oaths or blasphemies set in Qq not usually set by modern texts
SD	stage directions added or altered by modern texts
SP	a solo split line for a single character (see pp. xv–xvi above)

SPD	matters concerning songs, poems, or doggerel
?ST	where, because of question marks within the passage, the final choice as to the number of sentences is left to the reader's discretion
STRUCT	a deliberate change from the F1 setting by these texts
UE	an unusual entrance (set to the side of the text) or exit (set on a separate line)
VP	F1's verse altered to prose or vice versa, or lines indistinguishable as either
W	F1's word or phrase altered by modern texts
WHO	(in a convoluted passage) who is speaking to whom
WS	F1 line structure altered because of casting off problems (see pp. x–xi above)

FOOTNOTE CODING BY TOPIC

Stage Directions, etc.

A	asides
P	change in prefix assigned to a character
SD	stage directions added or altered by modern texts
UE	an unusual entrance (set to the side of the text) or exit (set on a separate line)
WHO	(in a convoluted passage) who is speaking to whom

Line Structure and Punctuation, etc.

L	letter or letters
LS	alterations in line structure
M	Shakespeare's use of the scansion of magic (trochaic and seven syllables)
PCT	alterations to F1's punctuation by modern and/or contemporary texts
SPD	matters concerning songs, poems, or doggerel
?ST	where, because of question marks within the passage, the final choice as to the number of sentences is left to the reader's discretion
SP	a solo split line for a single character (see pp. xv–xvi above)
VP	F1's verse altered to prose or vice versa, or lines indistinguishable as either

| WS | F1 line structure altered because of casting off problems (see pp. x–xi above) |

CHANGES TO WORDS AND PHRASES

AB	abbreviation
F	concerning disputed facts within the play
FL	foreign language
N	a name modern texts have changed or corrected for easier recognition
O	F1 words or phrases substituted for a Qq oath or blasphemy
QO	oaths or blasphemies set in Qq not usually set by modern texts
W	F1's word or phrase altered by modern texts

CHANGES ON A LARGER SCALE AND OTHER UNAUTHORISED CHANGES

ADD	a passage modern texts have added to their texts from F2–4/Qq
ALT	a passage (including act and scene division) that has been altered by modern texts without any Ff/Qq authority
COMP	a setting probably influenced by compositor interference
OM	passage, line, or word modern texts omit or suggest omitting
Q	material rejected or markedly altered by Qq not usually set by modern texts
STRUCT	a deliberate change from the F1 setting by these texts

ONE MODERN CHANGE FREQUENTLY NOTED IN THESE TEXTS

'MINUTE' CHANGES TO THE SYLLABLE LENGTH OF FF LINES

As noted above on pages xi–xii, modern texts frequently correct what commentators consider to be large scale metric deficiencies, often to the detriment of character and scene. There are many smaller changes made too, especially when lines are either longer or shorter than the norm of pentameter by 'only' one or two syllables. These changes are equally troublesome, for there is a highly practical theatrical rule of thumb guideline to such irregularities, viz.:

> if lines are slightly **longer** than pentameter, then the characters so involved have too much information coursing through them to be contained within the 'norms' of proper verse, occasionally even to the point of losing self-control

> if lines are slightly **shorter** than ten syllables, then either the information therein contained or the surrounding action is creating a momentary (almost need to breath) hesitation, sometimes suggesting a struggle to maintain self-control

These texts will note all such alterations, usually offering the different syllable counts per line as set both by F1 and by the altered modern texts, often with a brief suggestion as to how the original structural 'irregularity' might reflect onstage action.

FINALLY, A BRIEF WORD ABOUT THE COMPOSITORS [9]

Concentrated research into the number of the compositors and their habits began in the 1950s and, for a while, it was thought five men set the First Folio, each assigned a letter, 'A' through 'E'.

'E' was known to be a seventeen-year-old apprentice whose occasional mishaps both in copying text and securing the type to the frame have led to more than a few dreadful lapses, notably in *Romeo and Juliet*, low in the left column on p. 76 of the Tragedies, where in sixteen F1 lines he commits seven purely typographical mistakes. Compositor 'B' set approximately half of F1, and has been accused of being cavalier both with copying text and not setting line ending punctuation when the line is flush to the column edge. He has also been accused of setting most of the so called 'solo' split lines, though a comparison of other compositors' habits suggests they did so too, especially the conglomerate once considered to be the work of a single compositor known as 'A'. It is now acknowledged that the work set by 'A' is probably the work of at least two and more likely five different men, bringing the total number of compositors having worked on F1 to nine ('A' times five, and 'B' through 'E').

It's important to recognise that the work of these men was sometimes flawed. Thus the footnotes in these texts will point the reader to as many examples as possible which current scholarship and research suggest are in error. These errors fall into two basic categories. The first is indisputable, that of pure typographical mistakes ('wh?ch' for 'which'): the second, frequently open to challenge, is failure to copy exactly the text (Qq or manuscript) which F1 has used as its source material.

As for the first, these texts place the symbol † before a footnote marker within the text (not in the footnote section), a combination used only to point to a purely typographical mistake. Thus in the error-riddled section of *Romeo and Juliet* quoted above, p. 109 of this script shows fourteen footnote markers, seven of them coupled with the symbol †. Singling out these typographical-only markers alerts the reader to compositor error, and that (usually) the 'correct' word or phrase has been set within the text. Thus the reader doesn't have to bother with the footnote below unless they have a morbid curiosity to find out what the error actually is. Also, by definition, the more † appearing in a passage, the worse set that passage is.

As to the second series of (sometimes challengeable) errors labelled poor copy work, the footnotes will alert the reader to the alternative Qq word or phrase usage preferred by most modern texts, often discussing the alternatives in detail, especially when there seems to be validity to the F1 setting.

---

[9] Readers are directed to the ground breaking work of Alice Walker, and also to the ongoing researches of Paul Werstine and Peter W. M. Blayney.

Given the fluid state of current research, more discoveries are bound to be published as to which compositor set which F1 column long after these texts go to print. Thus the current assignation of compositors at the bottom of each of these scripts' pages represents what is known at this moment, and will be open to reassessment as time goes by.

A CAVEAT: THE COMPOSITORS AND 'SINGLE SPLIT LINES' (SEE PP. XV–XVI)

Many commentators suggest single split lines are not Shakespearean dramatic necessity, but compositorial invention to get out of a typesetting dilemma. Their argument is threefold:

first, as mentioned on pp. x–xi, because of 'white space' a small amount of text would have to be artificially expanded to fill a large volume of what would otherwise be empty space: therefore, even though the column width could easily accommodate regular verse lines, the line or lines would be split in two to fill an otherwise embarrassing gap

second, even though the source documents the compositors were using to set F1 showed material as a single line of verse, occasionally there was too much text for the F1 column to contain it as that one single line: hence the line had to be split in two

third, the device was essentially used by compositor B.

There is no doubt that sometimes single split lines did occur for typesetting reasons, but it should be noted that:

single split lines are frequently set well away from white space problems

often the 'too-much-text-for-the-F1-column-width' problem is solved by setting the last one or two words of the overly lengthy line either as a new line, or as an overflow or underflow just above the end of the existing line without resorting to the single split line

all compositors seem to employ the device, especially the conglomerate known as 'A' and compositor E.

As regards the following text, while at times readers will be alerted to the fact that typographical problems could have had an influence on the F1 setting, when single split lines occur their dramatic potential will be discussed, and readers are invited to explore and accept or reject the setting accordingly.

INTRODUCTION TO THE TEXT OF
THE LIFE AND DEATH OF KING JOHN [1]
pages 1 - 22 of the History Section [2]
All Act, Scene, and line numbers will refer to the
Applause text below unless otherwise stated.

Current research places the play between number four and twelve in the canon. It was set in tandem with *The Life and death of King Richard the Second,* and before the last two comedies, *Twelfe Night, Or what you will* and *The Winters Tale.*

Since the play contains no significant contemporary political references, two widely distinct dates are offered for composition, post Holinshed (the enlarged and reprinted Chronicles published 1587) and pre Meres (1598).[3] Because of the close structural association with an anonymous and virulently anti-Catholic two part play *The Troublesome Raigne of John, King of England* (1591) and a possible reference to Thomas Kyd's 1589 play *The Spanish Tragedy,* many commentators place the composition between 1590 - 1. The more current view, especially because of various linguistic tests and (perhaps) the notion that Constance's passion at the loss of her son (and his subsequent death) is a form of catharsis for Shakespeare who lost his son Hamnet in August 1596, places composition between 1596 and 1597.

SCHOLARS' ASSESSMENT

F1 is the sole authoritative text, and there's much debate as to its source. If foul papers,[4] there's very little accompanying confusion, if from the Playhouse there's very little of the theatrical, no music cues, and a lot of prefix changes, especially for John's Mother. With proof positive of two scribes established by the scholar Alice Walker, present conjecture is that F1 is

---

[1] For a detailed examination, see Wells, Stanley and Taylor, Gary (eds.). *William Shakespeare: A Textual Companion.* Oxford: Clarendon Press. 1987. pages 317 - 322: for a detailed analysis of the play's contents, see any of the Recommended Modern Texts.

[2] *Mr. William Shakespeare's Comedies, Histories, & Tragedies, 1623.*

[3] Holinshed, Raphael. *Chronicles Of England, Scotland And Ireland.* 1587 (2nd. edition): 1598 Francis Meres registered his *Palladis Tamia: Wit's Treasury* which, among many other items, listed this, if not all the Shakespeare plays that had been written pre-1598.

[4] In this and the next two paragraphs the following terms are used: 'foul papers', which refers to Shakespeare's first draft, with all the original crossings out and blots intact; 'prompt copy', which is a manuscript prepared by the Playhouse (copied from either fair or foul papers) with detailed information added necessary for staging a theatrical performance; 'bad quarto', which is one prepared without the full authority of the Playhouse (or individual) owning the copyright, and is often much at odds with what scholars regard as the 'legitimate' Shakespeare text.

based on a scribal copy prepared for future theatre use, itself taken from foul papers. The theory that the last two Acts were checked against a prompt-book is given little credence.

The question of whether *The Troublesome Raigne* was a Bad Quarto or whether it followed the Shakespeare play [5] and the differences between the two plays is discussed at length in the Appendix to *The New Cambridge Shakespeare King John*, pages 194 - 210, see Recommended Texts at the end of this introduction.

THE TEXT

was set by compositors B (24 columns) and C (20), with far fewer difficulties than editors seem to find in most other plays, except for the huge gap at the foot of L13 caused by problems in casting off. *A Textual Companion* lists just seven passages involving only twelve lines that needed to be altered for *The Oxford Shakespeares*.[6] Most critical scorn is reserved for what is often called the 'preposterous' Act and Scene Division, and the problems of Hubert.

CRITICAL ASSAULTS ON F1'S STAGE MANAGEMENT OF THE PLAY

With one exception, the stage management of the play is much better than many modern editors give it credit.

ADMITTEDLY, F1'S ACT AND SCENE DIVISION IS ALL OVER THE PLACE

- F1 divides its Actus Primus into two scenes, the second of which most modern texts rename Act Two Scene 1.
- F1's Act Two is then reset as Act Three, Scene One.
- F1's Actus Tertius Scæna Prima is usually set as a continuation of the modern Act Three Scene 1; its Scene Two is split into Scenes 2 and 3, and its Scene Three becomes the modern texts' Scene 4.
- Then there are the two F1 Actus Quartus (and no fifth act)! The first, page 54, is not altered by modern texts, while the second, page 75, is where the modern Act Five starts, and the scene breakdown for both is kept as is.

---

[5] Late twentieth century critical opinion is divided according to which date of Shakespearean composition is preferred; thus *A Textual Companion* suggests *The Troublesome Raigne* is a source but not a bad quarto since only one line is shared between them; *The New Cambridge Shakespeare* believes *The Troublesome Raigne* is a later imitation.

[6] Wells, Stanley and Taylor, Gary (eds.). *The Oxford Shakespeare, William Shakespeare, The Complete Works, Original Spelling Edition/Modern Spelling Edition*. Oxford: The Clarendon Press. 1986

THE UNNECESSARY SLAMMING OF THE PREFIXES

Some commentators have foolishly lambasted them as being incompetently set because of their supposed untidiness, when in fact a little theatrical imagination will open the reader up to the splendid theatrical possibilities.

• THE TWO PHILIPS

There is a supposed confusion between the French King Philip, and the putative anti-hero of the play, the English Philip Faulconbridge, who by the end of the first scene becomes known as the Bastard as soon as he joyously embraces the fact he is really the illegitimate son of the former English King, Richard Cordelion. Historically, the names are correct, so the confusion is hardly Shakespeare's, and when the characters appear on-stage together the English Philip's prefix is Bastard throughout, while the French moves between France and King.

• HOW BRASH IS THE KING OF FRANCE'S SON, LEWIS THE DOLPHIN?

Greater exception is taken to the fact that F1's prefix used to open the first formal greetings between the allies France and Austria, (the opening speeches, page 11), is not that of the French King but his son Lewis, also known as the Dolphin. Many commentators feel outraged by this and assign the speeches to the French Philip instead, totally spoiling two key character understandings. The first is that the son Lewis is a hot-head, constantly bucking protocol and authority, as is clearly shown when he defies Pandulph and the Pope in refusing to withdraw his forces from England. The second, as will be noted in the unnecessary punctuation changes page xlvi, is that King Philip may not be particularly competent.

• WHO IS HUBERT? WHAT IS HE ?

Even more is made of the problem of whether the 1st Citizen of Angiers/Anjou is also the character known as Hubert, over which there has been interminable discussion. The problem is, as the Trumpet sounds on page 18, a 'Citizen' appears, who is so prefixed up to the moment the rival forces go offstage to fight. On their return, the Citizen has disappeared and a character known as Hubert takes up the negotiations (page 22), and eventually becomes John's confidant.

Some commentators insist F1 is mistaken and that the Citizen and Hubert are one and the same character, and set their texts accordingly, others support F1 in that they indeed should be treated as two separate entities, and set their texts accordingly. [7] One of the most practical suggestions is that the two characters were originally doubled by the same actor.

---

[7] For an intriguing suggestion as to how the confusion might have arisen see *The New Cambridge Shakespeare King John*, pages 190 - 1.

• **THE ELEANOR VARIATIONS**

The character, King John's wily politico mother, is given four different prefixes. As they switch back and forth, they seem to underline her diplomatic skills so essential to her son, which might explain why John is so diplomatically stupid and politically inept after her death. 'Eleanor' seems to cover her more relaxed-with-family-and-comfortable-court situations; 'Queen' is applied when she verbally fights Constance and the French; 'Queen Mother' is used when she attempts to woo young Arthur away from his mother Constance; 'Old Queen' is applied as she advises John to accept the proposed marriage of convenience for his niece Blanche and the French Dolphin as a peaceful conclusion to what could be a devastating war.

• **MOST MODERN TEXTS' RESPONSE TO VARIATIONS, AND TO NAMES IN GENERAL**

Needless to say, no modern text sets these variations, nor the equally theatrical shifts between public and private persona offered for the Dolphin (Lewis and Dolphin); the English Philip (Philip and the Bastard) - though interestingly the French Philip is allowed no private side (King and France), as is John (King, King John, and John).

There are the usual Qq/Ff unspecified number of supernumeraries which cause little or no problem, save for the fact of how many executioners there might be assisting Hubert (page 54). The stage direction simply suggests 'Executioners', while the two prefixes are set as 'Exec.' which could be plural or singular. Again, footnotes will be offered when warranted.

Also, as with most history plays, F1's setting of people and places is sometimes at odds with either its source materials or current practice. Thus modern texts either modernise, or go back to the historically correct names. For readers wanting more detail, this text, as with all others in the History portion of this series, will make note of the more significant changes by setting a footnote marker plus † as they occur.

THE NOT ALWAYS COMPLETE STAGE DIRECTIONS

They offer the usual panoply of being fully complete to needing some form of expansion, for, as usual in an F1 (or Qq) play, quite a few of them are simply implied in the dialogue rather than being spelled out. This would have presented no problem to the original actors and prompt book holder, for it was second nature for them to fill in many of the smaller details without extra annotation. Whatever minor moments did not make their way to the various publishing houses were not added by the publishers since, as often as not, they weren't really missing if the text in question was closely followed. Thus in many of the scenes, a reader can get by without such directions simply by paying careful attention to the action of the play as the dialogue unfolds. (However, when the action remains obscure, this text, as all others in this series, will add extra information via footnotes.)

Sometimes the dialogue provides the explanation, as with Arthur's reference to his hoped-for-help to escape, 'This Ship-boyes semblance hath disguis'd me quite.', (line 4. 3. 4, page 69). Questions will always remain as to how the dying Meloon arrives to warn the rebellious English to abandon Lewis (page 85) and how the dying John is brought on-stage (page 91) - the latter usually on a 'litter' according to most modern texts, though F1 offers no explanation. Doubt will also remain as to how Essex knows simply from the entry of the Sheriffe (page 2, pre line 1. 1. 45) that the 'strangest controversie' of the two Faulconbridge brothers awaits John's intervention - does the Sheriffe whisper to him, pass him a note or is it all pre-arranged? Modern texts rightfully point out that the opening dialogue of the 'incorrect' second Actus Quartus (page 75) requires much more ceremony than F1 offers, and have creatively offered several solutions - see footnote #3 on that page. They also point out that though the general Exeunt is set on page 21 it is simply the English, French and Austrian forces who exit to fight off-stage, while the Citizen(s) stay securely on the walls to watch.

ASIDES [8]

These present little problem, with the English Philip functioning as a commentator throughout, especially during much of the verbal sparring before and after the various skirmishes in front of Angiers/Anjou, though the question arises whether some of the so-called asides are not meant to be heard by all around him. Thus the broadly sexual innuendo in response to his brother's rather dubious claim to the family title being based on King John's father's employment of their father

> Well sir, by this you cannot get my land,
> Your tale must be how he employ'd my mother.
> (page 5, lines 1. 1. 99 - 100)

is surely meant for the whole court, not just for himself as some modern texts suggest.

ENTRIES AND EXITS

These are sufficiently detailed, although questions are often raised as to whether F1's marked Actus Tertius really is a new scene and modern texts amend the stage directions accordingly - see footnotes #4 to page 33 and #2 page 34 for further details.

However, in the name of tidying, some modern texts play around with the timing of certain entries, often to the detriment of the on-stage action. Thus the occasional, apparently early, setting of an entry may not simply be a warning cue, as suggested for the Messenger, page 63 (see footnote #2), who most modern texts suggest, comes in at least two and a half lines too

---

[8] Asides are lines spoken by one character either directly to the audience, or to a small sub-group within a larger group on-stage, and not meant to be heard by anyone else. These are usually modern text additions, for Q/F rarely set such indications.

soon. In fact the timing, and the 'self-effacing' quality of the side-set entry,[9] suggests the character is in a quandary as to what to do since John is so upset by the departure of the soon to be rebellious nobles angered by the death of young Arthur. And the late entry of Lady Faulconbridge (bottom of page 8) has its theatrical place too, for it allows Philip, now prefixed as Bastard, to greet her before she arrives on-stage, thus immediately taking charge of the situation. Most modern texts advance her entry by two lines, thus putting her, rather than her son, in the ascendant.

MODERN INTERVENTIONS

Since the whole play is set in verse, the only variations in verse and prose would come about through the occasional verse line starting (accidentally) with lower case type. Such is the case with John's fourth line at the first confrontation with France, following their offstage skirmish (page 22, line 1. 2. 352) starting 'with course disturb'd' in an otherwise obvious verse speech.

OCCASIONAL IRREGULAR LINES AS A (POSSIBLE) SIGN OF PUBLIC AWKWARDNESS

Being a fairly early play, there are relatively few irregular verse lines, thus modern texts have made few alterations to F1.[10] Unfortunately, those lines that have been changed undo the crack in F1's normally formal diplomatic-guarded-verse-correctness of public conversation. Thus the F1 explosion given to the Bastard directed at Hubert over the death of Arthur

> Here's a good world: knew you of this faire work?
> Beyond the infinite and boundlesse reach of mercie, (13)
> (If thou didst this deed of death) art ÿ damn'd Hubert. (12)
> (page 73, lines 4. 2. 124 - 6)

becomes, according to the modern texts, a much more controlled

---

[9] Most F1 entries are set centered on a line separate from the surrounding dialogue. This entry is set as an exit (to the right of the text, on the same line as the dialogue that precedes it), and since crammed space is not responsible for the setting it is possible that it might signify either the entering character does not wish to draw attention to itself or that the reaction of those on-stage is equally important as the entry itself.

[10] It's useful to remember irregular lines do not dictate how a character should speak, but simply suggest that the character cannot speak pure poetry at that particular moment. The irregularities are not 'hopelessly corrupt' but occur where the reader would not expect the character(s) to be capable of speaking rationally or 'normally' or 'poetically' because of the inordinate strain they are undergoing. As such, great theatrical attention ought to be paid to them. (The short, less than ten syllable lines do not suggest that the character must pause for the full value of the 'silent' or missing syllables - they merely indicate that the character is incapable of finishing a line. Similarly, the long lines do not suggest the character should gabble or yell so as to get all the syllables into what would be a ten syllable line, just that the moment they are undergoing is so complex emotionally and/or intellectually that it cannot be fitted within the confines of a normal poetic line.)

Here's a good world: knew you of this faire work?
Beyond the infinite and boundlesse reach   (10)
Of mercie, (if thou didst this deed of death)   (10)
Art ÿ damn'd Hubert.   (4 + following as a split line)

Then there is the moment when the French-prince-who-came-to-fight-the enemy-England is suddenly side-tracked and fobbed off with an English related bride who then demands he doesn't fight against England even though honour (the support of Constance and Arthur) and religious dictates (the Pope's demand through Pandulph) demand he should. The gap (as marked by the *) between the demand of his wife, Blanche, and Constance's equally passionate demand

{Blanche}   Upon my knee I beg, goe not to Armes   (10)
              Against mine Uncle.   (5)*

Constance   O, upon my knee made hard with kneeling,   (10)
              I do pray to thee, thou vertuous Daulphin   (10-11)
                          (page 41, lines 3. 1. 245 - 48)

speaks volumes as to his dilemma. The usual resetting, establishing shared lines,

{Blanche}   Upon my knee I beg, goe not to Armes
              Against mine Uncle.

Constance   O, upon my knee   (10)
              Made hard with kneeling, I do pray to thee,   (10)
              Thou vertuous Daulphin . . .

replaces the awkward Dolphin focused silent non-response with another on-going verbal attack of the never-ending Constance. F1, in allowing her to see his wavering before skillfully trying to exploit the perceived weakness, suggests a very skillful operator, so much more than the shrill harridan most modern texts and productions present.

Most of the single split lines [11] are probably occasioned by a lack of column width. However, if they are allowed to stand, some lovely personal moments arise, such as John's extraordinarily quick decision to knight the English Philip, thus acknowledging him a (illegitimate) royal relative

King John   From henceforth beare his name   (6)
              Whose forme thou bearest: (5)
                          (page 7, lines 1. 1. 162 - 3)

and allowing a silent moment of choice before, or a stunned response after, before continuing

Kneele thou downe Philip, but rise more great

---

[11]   These are two or more short verse lines, set for a single character, which if placed together (as poets, scholars and commentators suggest), would form a single full line of verse. These lines are rarely reproduced as set by any modern text : see the General Introduction, pages xv - xvi for further discussion.

MODERN PUNCTUATION TIDYING, UNDOING (POSSIBLE) F1 UNCERTAINTY

It is the punctuation that has been most altered, all in the name of grammatical accuracy, which in turn has butchered some highly effective theatrical breaks in formal composure. Sometimes a genuine cry for help such as that of the King of France, suddenly faced with being plunged back into war with England because of the Pope's demand for King John to be excommunicated, when he asks the papal Legate, Pandulph,

> Good reverend father, make my person yours,
> And tell me how you would bestow your selfe?
> >   (page 39, lines 3. 1. 156 - 7)

is turned into arrogant posturing, here simply by changing F1's question mark to a period, 'bestow your selfe'.

Sometimes a character which is not at all at ease, as France when he finally opens his mouth to the assembled allies

> Well, then to worke our Canon shall be bent
> Against the browes of this resisting towne,
> Call for our cheefest men of discipline
> >   (page 12, lines 1. 2. 37 - 39)

is made to appear much more coherent by judicious repunctuation, with the commonly accepted modern reworking

> Well* then,* to worke;* our Canon shall be bent
> Against the browes of this resisting towne.*
> Call for our cheefest men of discipline

the asterisks noting the modern changes. The modern France is in charge, the F1 one clearly out of his depth.

Similar problems arise out of 'correcting' Constance's run-ons once she hears of the farce of the politically arranged marriage which denotes the dashing of all her French and Austrian support (page 33, line 2. 1. 72, starting with 'Thou maist . . .').

Indeed such pettifogging adjustments have served to mask much of the humanity that peeps through the rhetorical cracks that puncture the facade of public behaviours in this play. Thus John's final triumphant flourish of a new sentence as to why the Citizens of Angiers/Anjou should accept him as their monarch

> . . . accordingly kinde Cittizens,
> And let us in.* Your King, whose labour'd spirits
> >   (page 19, lines 1. 2. 238 - 40)

has been reduced to mere continual debate by replacing the period with a colon, viz.

> . . . accordingly kinde Cittizens,
> And let us in: * your King, whose labour'd spirits

THE OCCASIONAL MOMENTS OF DEBATE

• DEBATE DAMAGED BY FUSSY REPUNCTUATION

This can ruin the debate quality of the play - after all diplomacy is full of control and the occasional tiny crack, not a loud and extravagant yell, except when deliberately required. Careful self protection may be undermined, as with F1's Hubert obviously giving nothing away as King John orders the death of Arthur. Hubert's non-committal 'My Lord.' is a far cry from most modern texts 'My Lord?': the modern substitution of the question mark creating a totally different response.

Dignity, such as Salisbury's abandoning his King over Arthur's death

> It is apparant foule-play, and 'tis shame
> That Greatnesse should so grossely offer it;
> So thrive it in your game, and so farewell.
>
> (page 63, lines 4. 2. 93 - 5)

can be ruined by the substitution of the overworked exclamation point

> It is apparant foule-play, and 'tis shame
> That Greatnesse should so grossely offer it;
> So thrive it in your game!* and so farewell.

and emotional upset, such as the Bastard's uncharacteristic grammatical breakdown as the body of young Arthur is carried off-stage

> How easie dost thou take all England up,*
> From forth this morcell of dead Royaltie?*
> The life, the right, and truth of all this Realme
> Is fled to heaven; and England now is left
>
> (page 74, lines 154 - 7)

becomes so much more predictable with the modern texts'

> How easie dost thou take all England up!*
> From forth this morcell of dead Royaltie,*
> The life, the right, and truth of all this Realme
> Is fled to heaven; and England now is left

which replaces nigh near incoherence with the traditional emotional release of the exclamation point, followed by the logical comma at the end of the next line.

• DEBATE AND SHARED SPLIT LINES [12]

Even though an early play, Spevack[13] suggests there are 69 shared split lines the largest number (14 each) going to the two characters with the most conscience, Hubert and Philip the bastard.

---

[12] Two or more short verse lines, set for <u>two or more</u> characters, which if placed together would form one full line of verse: see the General Introduction, pages xii - xv for further discussion.

[13] Spevack, M. *A Complete And Systematic Concordance To The Works Of Shakespeare.* (9 vols.) Hildesheim. Georg Holms. 1968 - 1980

FACTS

In *Casting Shakespeare's Plays* T.J. King [14] suggests there are 2,640 spoken lines and that ten actors can play twelve principal roles. Five boys can play four principal female roles and the two Princes, Arthur and Henry. Nine men can play nine smaller speaking roles and twenty-seven mutes.

The 'CATALOGUE' lists the play as *The Life and Death of King John,* the header and the title above the text is *The life and death of King John.* The pages are numbered correctly. There are two catch word variations.

For the horrors of the F1 Act and scene division, and modern revisions, see page xl above. From page 75 on, the symbols 4* in the top of the page line numbering will distinguish the second Actus Quartus from the first, which starts on page 54.

Neil Freeman,
Vancouver, B.C.
Canada, 1999

---

[14]   King, T.J. *Casting Shakespeare's Plays.* Cambridge. Cambridge University Press. 1992

RECOMMENDED MODERN TEXTS WITH EXCELLENT SCHOLARLY FOOTNOTES AND RESEARCH

The footnotes in this text are concise, and concentrate either on matters theatrical or choices in word or line structure which distinguish most modern editions and this Folio based text. Items of literary, historical, and linguistic concern have been well researched and are readily available elsewhere. One of the best **research** works in recent years is

Wells, Stanley, and Gary Taylor, eds. *William Shakespeare: A Textual Companion*. Oxford: Clarendon Press, 1987.

In terms of modern **texts,** readers are urged to consult at least one of the following:

Evans, Gwynne Blakemore, Harry Levin, Anne Barton, Herschel Baker, Frank Kermode, Hallet D. Smith, and Marie Edel, eds. *The Riverside Shakespeare*. Copyright © 1974 by Houghton Mifflin Company.

Honigmann, E. A. J. (ed.). *King John*. The Arden Shakespeare. 1954

Beaurline, L. A. (ed.). *King John*. The New Cambridge Shakespeare. 1990

Dramatis Personæ

The English Court
KING JOHN
his mother, ELEANOR
his neece, Lady BLANCHE

Earle of SALISBURY
Earle of PEMBROKE
Earle of ESSEX
Lord BIGOT

Petitioners To The Court
Philip the BASTARD, illegitimate son of Richard 1st.
ROBERT Faulconbridge, his legitimate brother
their Mother, LADY Faulconbridge
James GURNIE, her attendant

Claimant To The English Throne
ARTHUR, Duke of Brittaine, King John's nephew
his mother, Lady CONSTANCE

Supporters Of Arthur's Claim
KING Philip, of France
his son, Lewis the DOLPHIN
The Duke of AUSTRIA (also known as Lymoges)
CHATILLION, the French Ambassador
a soldier, Count MELOONE

From The Pope
the Legate, Cardinal PANDULPH

a CITIZEN of Angiers
HUBERT, of Angiers, later a confidant to King John
EXECUTIONERS
a prophet, PETER of Pomfret
HERALDS
MESSENGERS
a SHERIFFE

Lords, Attendants, Souldiers

This Cast List has been specially prepared for this edition, and will not be found in the Facsimile

The life and death of King John

Actus Primus, Scæna Prima

ENTER KING JOHN, QUEENE ELINOR, PEMBROKE, ESSEX, AND SA-
LISBURY, WITH THE CHATTYLION [1] OF FRANCE [2]

King John	Now[†] say Chatillion, what would France with us?
Chattilion	Thus (after greeting) speakes the King
	of France,
	In my behaviour to the Majesty,
5		The borrowed Majesty of England heere.
Eleanor	A strange beginning : borrowed Majesty?
King John	Silence (good mother) heare the Embassie.
Chatillion	Philip of France, in right and true behalfe
	Of thy deceased brother, Geffreyes sonne,
10		Arthur Plantaginet, laies most lawfull claime
	To this faire Iland, and the Territories :
	To Ireland, Poyctiers, Anjowe, Torayne,[3] Maine,
	Desiring thee to lay aside the sword
	Which swaies usurpingly these severall titles,
15		And put the same into yong Arthurs hand,
	Thy Nephew, and right royall Soveraigne.
King John	What followes if we disallow of this?

[N/P 1] this stage direction shows the name 'Chattylion', the opening dialogue the name 'Chatillion', the prefix 'Chat.', the next full stage direction (page 12 this text) 'Chattilion', all of which most modern texts set as 'Chatillon': this text will use the prefix 'Chatillion', as he is first named by King John

[SD 2] most modern texts add Attendants to the entry

[N 3] most modern texts set the current spelling of these place names, viz. 'Poitiers', 'Anjou' and 'Touraine': this is the only time these variations will be noted

1

Chatillion	The proud contröle of fierce and bloudy warre,
	To inforce these rights, so forcibly with-held,[1]
20 King John	Heere have we war for war, & bloud for bloud,
	Controlement for controlement:[2] so answer France.
Chatillion	Then take my Kings defiance from my mouth,
	The farthest limit of my Embassie.
King John	Beare mine to him, and so depart in peace,
25	Be thou as lightning in the eies of France;
	For ere thou canst report, I will be there:
	The thunder of my Cannon shall be heard.
	So hence: be thou the trumpet of our wrath,
	And sullen presage of your owne decay:
30	An honourable conduct let him have,
	Pembroke looke too't: farewell Chattillion.

[Exit Chat.{illion} and Pem.{broke}]

Eleanor	What now my sonne, have I not ever said
	How that ambitious Constance would not cease
	Till she had kindled France and all the world,
35	Upon the right and party of her sonne.
	This might have beene prevented, and made whole
	With very easie arguments of love,
	Which now the manage of two kingdomes must
	With fearefull bloudy issue arbitrate.
40 King John	Our strong possession, and our right for us.
Eleanor	Your strong possession much more then your right,
	Or else it must go wrong with you and me,
	So much my conscience whispers in your eare, L1 - c
	Which none but heaven, and you, and I, shall heare.

ENTER A SHERIFFE [3]

45 Essex	My Liege, here is the strangest controversie
	Come from the Country to be judg'd by you
	That ere I heard: shall I produce the men?

[PCT] [1] F1 sets a comma as if Chatillion interrupts him: F2/most modern texts set a period

[W] [2] Ff/some modern texts = 'Controlement for controlement', some modern texts = 'Controlement for control',
which answers both the needs of meter and meaning (see *The New Cambridge Shakespeare King John*, page 64,
footnote to line 20, for further details)

[SD] [3] since Essex rather than the Sheriffe announces the request for judgement, most modern texts indicate the Sheriffe
passes information on to Essex, either via a paper, or by whispering to him

King John	Let them approach : [1]	
50	Our Abbies and our Priories shall pay	
	This expeditious[2] charge : what men are you?	

[3] **ENTER ROBERT FAULCONBRIDGE, AND PHILIP** [4]

Philip Your faithfull subject, I [5] a gentleman,
Borne in Northamptonshire, and eldest sonne
As I suppose, to Robert Faulconbridge,
A Souldier by the Honor-giving-hand
55 Of Cordelion,[6] Knighted in the field.

King John What art thou?

Robert The son and heire to that same Faulconbridge.

King John Is that the elder, and art thou the heyre?
You came not of one mother then it seemes.

60 **Philip** Most certain of one mother, mighty King,
That is well knowne, and as I thinke one father :
But for the certaine[†7] knowledge of that truth,
I put you o're to heaven, and to my mother ;
Of that I doubt, as all mens children may.

65 **Eleanor** Out on thee rude man, ÿ [8] dost shame thy mother,
And wound her honor with this diffidence.

[SD 1] most modern texts indicate the Sheriffe leaves to get the men, and that he accompanies them back in

[W/PCT 2] F1 = 'expeditious', F2/most modern texts = 'expeditions': also, F1 sets a colon allowing King John to switch topics very quickly (perhaps something about the appearance of the two plaintiffs takes him by surprise, or as if he were playing with them: F2/most modern texts set a grammatically correct period

[SD 3] most modern texts advance the entry to before King John's question in the previous line

[P/N 4] as critics have noted, there are two Philip's in the play, the English Philip the Bastard who makes his entry now, and King Philip of France, who is first seen at the beginning of Act Two: even when they are on-stage at the same time there is no confusion of prefixes between characters, so for each character this script will use the appropriate F1 prefix as and when F1 sets it: for the English Philip most modern texts set Bastard throughout, which somewhat obscures the point that until he joins the Court he has an identity irrespective of his status, all of which changes once Eleanor and John 'adopt' him (see footnote #2 , page 6)

[PCT 5] some commentators very sniffily point to the supposedly appalling grammar of this setting, blaming the compositor for setting 'subject, I a gentleman,', replacing it with 'subject I, a gentleman': however, throughout Philip is a hot-headed breath of fresh air who speaks his mind, and the current need for judgement centres round the very fact of whether he is a 'gentleman' or not: the F1 setting may be grammatically horrible, but emotionally perfectly understandable

[N 6] Ff = 'Cordelion', some modern texts set the modern spelling 'Cœur-de-lion' throughout

[W 7] F2/most modern texts = 'certaine', F1 = 'cerraine'

[AB 8] F1 = 'ÿ', (printed as such because of lack of column width), F2/most modern texts = 'thou'

3

Philip	I Madame?
	No, I have no reason for it,
	That is my brothers plea, and none of mine,
70	The which if he can prove, a pops me out,
	At least from faire five hundred pound a yeere :
	Heaven guard my mothers honor, and my Land.
King John	A good blunt fellow : why being yonger born
	Doth he lay claime to thine inheritance?
75 **Philip**	I know not why, except to get the land :
	But once he slanderd me with bastardy :
	But [1] where I be as true begot or no,
	That still I lay upon my mothers head,
	But that I am as well begot my Liege
80	(Faire fall the bones that tooke the paines for me)
	Compare our faces, and be Judge your selfe [2]
	If old Sir Robert did beget us both,
	And were our father, and this sonne like him : [3]
	O old sir Robert Father, on my knee
85	I give heaven thankes I was not like to thee.
King John	Why what a mad-cap hath heaven lent us here?
Eleanor	He hath a tricke of Cordelions face,
	The accent of his tongue affecteth him :
	Doe you not read some tokens of my sonne
90	In the large composition of this man? R 1 - c
King John	Mine eye hath well examined his parts,
	And findes them perfect Richard : [4] sirra speake,
	What doth move you to claime your brothers land.
Philip	Because he hath a half-face like my father? [5]
95	With halfe that face would he have all my land,
	A halfe-fac'd groat, five hundred pound a yeere?

[W] [1]   since Ff's 'But' appears in the same position in the line above and in two lines time, some critics and at least one modern text suggest 'Now' here: again, Ff are perfectly understandable; a blunt man without much regard for rhetoric might well repeat a particular word several times in quick succession

[PCT] [2]   F1 sets no punctuation, allowing Philip to rush on cheerfully unchecked: most modern texts set a period

[PCT] [3]   Ff set a colon, allowing a slightly bigger build-up to the humorous and unruly put-down: grammatically concerned modern texts replace the colon with a comma

[WHO] [4]   most modern texts suggest this is spoken to Robert

[PCT] [5]   F1 sets a question mark, presumably being used in it's Elizabethan alternative function as an exclamation point: F2 sets a comma, some modern texts an exclamation point

Robert	My gracious Liege, when that my father liv'd,
	Your brother did imploy my father much.
Philip	[1] Well sir, by this you cannot get my land,
100	Your tale must be how he employ'd my mother.
Robert	And once dispatch'd him in an Embassie
	To Germany, there with the Emperor
	To treat of high affaires touching that time:
	Th'advantage of his absence tooke the King,
105	And in the meane time sojourn'd at my fathers;
	Where how he did prevaile, I shame to speake:
	But truth is truth, large lengths of seas and shores
	Betweene my father, and my mother lay,
	As I have heard my father speake himselfe
110	When this same lusty gentleman was got:
	Upon his death-bed he by will bequeath'd
	His lands to me, and tooke it on his death
	That this my mothers sonne was none of his;
	And if he were, he came into the world
115	Full fourteene weeks before the course of time:
	Then good my Liedge let me have what is mine,
	My fathers land, as was my fathers will.
King John	Sirra, your brother is Legittimate,
	Your fathers wife did after wedlocke beare him:
120	And if she did play false, the fault was hers,
	Which fault lyes on the hazards of all husbands
	That marry wives: tell me, how if my brother
	Who as you say, tooke paines to get this sonne,
	Had of your father claim'd this sonne for his,[2]
125	Insooth, good friend, your father might have kept
	This Calfe, bred from his Cow from all the world:
	Insooth he might: then if he were my brothers,
	My brother might not claime him, nor your father
	Being none of his, refuse him: this concludes,
130	My mothers sonne did get your fathers heyre,
	Your fathers heyre must have your fathers land.
Robert	Shal then my fathers Will be of no force,
	To dispossesse that childe which is not his.

[A][1] for some strange reason some modern texts suggest this is spoken as an aside, yet Philip's appeal to date is to be outspoken even in front of royalty: there seems to be no reason for him to become coy now

[PCT][2] most modern texts follow an early gloss and make the two and a half lines up to this point a question by setting a question mark: the firmness of the Ff setting as a statement seems perfectly acceptable as is

135	**Philip**	Of no more force to dispossesse me sir, Then was his will to get me, as I think.
	Eleanor	Whether hadst thou rather be a Faulconbridge, And like thy brother to enjoy thy land: ¹ Or the reputed sonne of Cordelion, Lord of thy presence, and no land beside.
140	Philip as **Bastard** ²	Madam, and if my brother had my shape And I had his, sir Roberts his like him, And if my legs were two such riding rods, My armes, such eele-skins stuft, my face so thin, That in mine eare I durst not sticke a rose,
145		Lest men should say, looke where three farthings goes, And to his shape were heyre to all this land, Would I might never stirre from off this place, I would give it every foot to have this face: It³ would not be sir nobbe in any case.
150	**Eleanor**	I like thee well: wilt thou forsake thy fortune, Bequeath thy land to him, and follow me? I am a Souldier, and now bound to France.
	Bastard	Brother, take you my land, Ile take my chance; Your face hath got five hundred pound a yeere,
155		Yet sell your face for five pence and 'tis deere: Madam, Ile follow you unto the death.
	Eleanor	Nay, I would have you go before me thither.
	Bastard	Our Country manners give our betters way.
	King John	What is thy name?
160	**Bastard**	Philip my Liege, so is my name begun. Philip, good old Sir Roberts wives eldest sonne.

L2 - c (at line 155)

L 2 - c / R 2 - c : 1. 1. 132 - 158

PCT ₁ once more the Ff punctuation is perfectly acceptable rhetorically, for it allows full weight to the moment as Eleanor begins to spell out the tantalising alternative: some modern texts set the passage grammatically, as shown below, thus reducing the drama of the moment

> Whether hadst thou rather be: a Faulconbridge,
> And like thy brother to enjoy thy land,
> Or the reputed sonne of Cordelion,
> Lord of thy presence and no land beside.

in addition, the removal of Ff's comma in the last line again somewhat diminishes Eleanor's spelling out the consequences of accepting the second alternative

P ₂ at the moment of choice , F1 quite wonderfully establishes what Philip is about to do by changing the prefix from his given name, by which he has been known so far, to that of the status he will have to acknowledge from now on: most modern texts set the prefix 'Bastard' throughout and do not show this moment of transition

▼ ₃ F2/most modern texts = 'I', F1 = 'It'

King John	From henceforth beare his name →[1]
	Whose forme thou bearest:
	Kneele thou downe Philip, but rise [2] more great,
165	Arise Sir Richard, and Plantagenet.

Bastard	Brother by th'mothers side, give me your hand,
	My father gave me honor, yours gave land:
	Now blessed be the houre by night or day
	When I was got, Sir Robert was away.

| 170 Eleanor | The very spirit of Plantaginet: |
| | I am thy grandame Richard, call me so. |

| Bastard | Madam by chance, but not by truth, what tho; |

[3] Something about [4] a little from the right,
In at the window, or else ore the hatch:
175   Who dares not stirre by day, must walke by night,
And have is have, how ever men doe catch:
Neere or farre off, well wonne is still well shot,
And I am I, how ere I was begot.

King John	Goe, Faulconbridge, now hast thou thy desire,
180	A landlesse Knight, makes thee a landed Squire:
	Come Madam, and come Richard, we must speed
	For France, for France, for it is more then need.

| Bastard | Brother adieu, good fortune come to thee, |
| | For thou wast got i'th way of honesty. |

[Exeunt all but bastard]

| 185 Bastard | A foot of Honor better then I was, |
| | But many a many foot of Land the worse. |

Well, now can I make any Joane a Lady,
Good den Sir Richard, Godamercy fellow,
And if his name be George, Ile call him Peter;
190   For new made honor doth forget mens names:

[SP] [1] the Ff only two short lines (6/5 syllables) probably came about because there was insufficient width in the F1 column to set the text as a single line: most modern texts join the two lines together

[LS] [2] the Ff nine syllable line allows a moment for John to minutely pause either through enjoyment of the moment or to begin the ritual of knighthood: at least one text suggests setting 'arise' instead of 'rise' , thus creating pentameter

[SPD] [3] since most of these lines echo Elizabethan maxims, at least one modern text insets the lines somewhat , presumably suggesting that they be spoken as poetry or doggerel

[W] [4] *The Arden Shakespeare King John*, op. cit., suggests setting 'above' for Ff's 'about' to explain and clarify the reference to illegitimacy: for further details see that text's page 70, footnotes to lines 170 - 5, and to line 170

'Tis two [1] respective, and too sociable
For your conversion, now your traveller,
Hee and his tooth-picke at my worships messe,
And when my knightly stomacke is suffis'd,
195   When then I sucke my teeth, and catechize
My picked man of Countries: my deare sir,
Thus leaning on mine elbow I begin,
I shall beseech [2] you; that is question now,
And then comes answer like an Absey booke:
200   O sir, sayes answer, at your best command,
At your employment, at your service sir:
No sir, saies question, I sweet sir at yours,
And so ere answer knowes what question would,
Saving in Dialogue of Complement,
205   And talking of the Alpes and Appenines,
The Perennean [3] and the river Poe,
It drawes toward supper in conclusion so.

But this is worshipfull society,
And fits the mounting spirit like my selfe;
210   For he is but a bastard to the time
That doth not smoake [4] of observation,
And so am I whether I smacke or no:
And not alone in habit and device,
Exterior forme, outward accoutrement;
215   But from the inward motion to deliver
Sweet, sweet, sweet poyson for the ages tooth,
Which though I will not practice to deceive,
Yet to avoid deceit I meane to learne;
For it shall strew the footsteps of my rising:
220   But who comes in such haste in riding robes?   R2 - c

What woman post is this? hath she no husband
That will take paines to blow a horne before her?

O me, 'tis my mother: how now good Lady,
What brings you heere to Court so hastily?

ENTER LADY FAULCONBRIDGE AND JAMES GURNEY [5]

---

[1] F2/most modern texts = 'too', F1 = 'two'

[2] F2/most modern texts = 'beseech', F1 = 'beseeeh'

[3] F2 - 4 = 'Pyrennean', which most modern texts set as 'Pyrenean', F1 = 'Perennean'

[4] Ff = 'smoake', most modern texts set 'smack'

[5] most modern texts advance the entry two lines so that his mother is on-stage before he talks to her: the Ff setting allows him to take the advantage by greeting her as she arrives

8

225	Lady	Where is that slave thy brother? where is he? That holds in chase mine honour up and downe.
	Bastard	My brother Robert, old Sir Roberts sonne: Colbrand the Gyant, that same mighty man, Is it Sir Roberts sonne that you seeke so?
230	Lady	Sir Roberts sonne, I thou unreverend boy, Sir Roberts sonne? why scorn'st thou at sir Robert? He is Sir Roberts sonne, and so art thou.
	Bastard	James Gournie, wilt thou give us leave a while?
	Gournie	Good leave good Philip.
235	Bastard	Philip, sparrow, James,[1] There's toyes abroad, anon Ile tell thee more.

[Exit James]

		Madam, I was not old Sir Roberts sonne, Sir Robert might have eat his part in me Upon good Friday, and nere broke his fast: Sir Robert could doe well, marrie to confesse
240		Could[2] get me sir Robert could not doe it;[3] We know his handy-worke, therefore good mother To whom am I beholding for these limmes? Sir Robert never holpe to make this legge. †[4]
245	Lady	Hast thou conspired with thy brother too, That for thine owne gaine shouldst defend mine honor? What meanes this scorne, thou most untoward knave?
	Bastard	Knight, knight good mother, Basilisco-like: What, I am dub'd, I have it on my shoulder:
250		But mother, I am not Sir Roberts sonne, I have disclaim'd Sir Robert and my land, Legitimation, name, and all is gone; Then good my mother, let me know my father, Some proper man I hope, who was it mother?

PCT/W [1]
most modern texts repunctuate with question and exclamation marks, viz. 'Philip? - sparrow! James . . .': the Ff setting allows for a far more casual dismissal, viz. 'Philip, sparrow, James': also, one excellent gloss offers 'spare me' for 'sparrow'

W [2]
most modern texts add 'he', Ff omit the word

PCT [3]
for grammatical clarity some modern texts set the Ff phrase 'sir Robert could not doe it' as a separate sentence: the Ff setting though grammatically sloppy underlines the nervous energy Philip must be undergoing as he tries to establish the possibility of Cordelion being his father

W [4]
F2 = 'legge', which most modern texts set as 'leg', F1 = 'leg ge'

255	Lady	Hast thou denied thy selfe a Faulconbridge?
	Bastard	As faithfully as I denie the devill.

	Lady	King Richard Cordelion was thy father,
		By long and vehement suit I was seduc'd
		To make roome for him in my husbands bed:
260		Heaven ¹ lay not my transgression to my charge,
		That art the issue of my deere offence
		Which was so strongly urg'd past my defence.

	Bastard	Now by this light were I to get againe,
		Madam I would not wish a better father:
265		Some sinnes doe beare their priviledge on earth,
		And so doth yours: your fault, was not your follie,
		Needs must you lay your heart at his dispose,
		Subjected tribute to commanding love,
		Against whose furie and unmatched force,
270		The awlesse Lion could not wage the fight,
		Nor keepe his Princely heart from Richards hand:
		He that perforce robs Lions of their hearts,
		May easily winne a womans: aye my mother,
		With all my heart I thanke thee for my father:
275		Who lives and dares but say, thou didst not well
		When I was got, Ile send his soule to hell.

		Come Lady I will shew thee to my kinne,
		And they shall say, when Richard me begot,
		If thou hadst sayd him nay, it had beene sinne;
280		Who sayes it was, he lyes, I say twas not.

[Exeunt]

L3 - c

---

^{PCT}₁ some modern texts make much more of Lady Faulconbridge's statement than Ff by adding an exclamation mark after 'Heaven!': as set, Ff allow her a dignified admission of her 'guilt'

Scæna Secunda
[Most modern texts rename this as Act Two, Scene 1]

ENTER BEFORE ANGIERS, PHILIP KING OF FRANCE, LEWIS,[1] DAUL-
PHIN, AUSTRIA, CONSTANCE, ARTHUR [2]

Lewis[3]　　Before Angiers well met brave Austria,
Arthur that great fore-runner of thy bloud,
Richard that rob'd the Lion of his heart,
And fought the holy Warres in Palestine,
5　　　　　　By this brave Duke came early to his grave :
And for amends to his posteritie,
At our importance hether is he come,
To spread his colours boy, in thy behalfe,
And to rebuke the usurpation
10　　　　　Of thy unnaturall Uncle, English John,
Embrace him, love him, give him welcome hether.

Arthur　　God shall forgive you Cordelions death
The rather, that you give his off-spring life,
Shadowing their right under your wings of warre :
15　　　　　I give you welcome with a powerlesse hand,
But with a heart full of unstained love,
Welcome before the gates of Angiers Duke.

Lewis　　A[4] noble boy, who would not doe thee right?

Austria　　Upon thy cheeke lay I this zelous kisse,
20　　　　　As seale to this indenture of my love :
That to my home I will no more returne
Till Angiers, and the right thou hast in France,

N/PCT [1] 'Lewis' is the 'Daulphin' (spelled 'Dolphin' in most modern texts), the hereditary title for the eldest son
of the King of France: thus most modern texts remove Ff's comma separating the names

SD [2] most modern texts suggest Philip and Lewis escort Constance and Arthur and enter through one door
accompanied by their soldiers, and that Austria enters similarly accompanied through the other

P [3] throughout the text Lewis the Dolphin is proven to be a hot-head: here, unequivocally, Ff set the opening speech
and next response for him rather than for Philip his father, the rather weak and vacillating King of France: however,
most modern texts seem to think this is an unseemly breech of protocol and set the speech for the father rather than
the son, which more than somewhat undermines the inner nature of the two men as shown later in the play

W [4] though Ff's 'A' is perfectly acceptable, one gloss = 'Ah,'

Together with that pale, that white-fac'd shore,
Whose foot spurnes backe the Oceans roaring tides,
25 And coopes from other lands her Ilanders,
Even till that England hedg'd in with the maine,
That Water-walled Bulwarke, still secure
And confident from forreine purposes,
Even till that utmost corner of the West
30 Salute thee for her King, till then faire boy
Will I not thinke of home, but follow Armes.

Constance O take his mothers thanks, a widdows thanks,
Till your strong hand shall helpe to give him strength,
To make a more requitall to your love.

35 **Austria** The peace of heaven is theirs ÿ [1] lift their swords
In such a just and charitable warre.

Philip of France as
King [2] Well, then to worke [3] our Cannon shall be bent
Against the browes of this resisting towne,
Call for our cheefest men of discipline,
40 To cull the plots of best advantages:
Wee'll lay before this towne our Royal bones,
Wade to the market-place in French-mens bloud,
But we will make it subject to this boy.

Constance Stay for an answer to your Embassie,
45 Lest unadvis'd you staine your swords with bloud,
My Lord Chattilion may from England bring
That right in peace which heere we urge in warre,
And then we shall repent each drop of bloud,
That hot rash haste so indirectly shedde.

ENTER CHATTILION

50 **King** A wonder Lady: lo upon thy wish
Our Messenger Chattilion is arriv'd,
What England saies, say breefely gentle Lord,
We coldly pause for thee, Chatilion speake, [4]

[AB] [1] F1 = 'ÿ', (printed as such because of lack of column width), F2/most modern texts = 'that'

[P] [2] unlike most modern texts, this is the first speech Ff assign to the King of France (see footnote #3, page 11): as
the following footnote shows, F1 - 3 suggest he doesn't handle the opening too successfully

[PCT] [3] F4 sets a comma, most modern texts some form of major punctuation: F1 - 3 set no punctuation, as if the first Ff
speech assigned the King suggests he is having difficulty handling the situation

[PCT] [4] F1 sets a comma, perhaps suggesting Chatillion, in his concern, interrupts his master: F2/most modern texts
set a period

12

Chatillion	Then turne your forces from this paltry siege,
55	And stirre them up against a mightier taske:
	England impatient of your just demands,
	Hath put himselfe in Armes, the adverse windes R3 - c
	Whose leisure I have staid, have given him time
	To land his Legions all as soone as I:
60	His marches are expedient to this towne,
	His forces strong, his Souldiers confident:
	With him along is come the Mother Queene,[1]
	An Ace[2] stirring him to bloud and strife,
	With her her Neece, the Lady Blanch of Spaine,
65	With them a Bastard of the Kings deceast,
	And all th'unsetled humors of the Land,
	Rash, inconsiderate, fiery voluntaries,
	With Ladies faces, and fierce Dragons spleenes,
	Have sold their fortunes at their native homes,
70	Bearing their birth-rights proudly on their backs,
	To make a hazard of new fortunes heere:
	In briefe, a braver choyse of dauntlesse spirits
	Then now the English bottomes have waft o're,
	Did never flote upon the swelling tide,
75	To doe offence and scathe in Christendome:
	The interruption of their churlish drums
	Cuts off more circumstance, they are at hand,

[Drum beats][3]

	To parlie or to fight, therefore prepare.
King	How much unlook'd for, is this expedition.
80 **Austria**	By how much unexpected, by so much
	We must awake indevor for defence,
	For courage mounteth with occasion,
	Let them be welcome then, we are prepar'd.

ENTER K.{ING} OF ENGLAND, BASTARD, QUEENE, BLANCH, PEMBROKE, AND OTHERS

King John	Peace be to France: If France in peace permit
85	Our just and lineall entrance to our owne;
	If not, bleede France, and peace ascend to heaven.[4]

R3 - c / L4 - c : 2. 1. 54 - 88

PCT [1] F4/some modern texts illustrate the compound epithet by setting a hyphen between the words, viz. 'Mother-Queene'

N [2] Ff = 'Ace', most modern texts set 'Ate', the Greek goddess of discord and mischief

SD [3] most modern texts advance the direction two lines, thus the drums are heard before Chatillion mentions them

PCT [4] F1 - 3 set a period, as if King John were taking great care to set up the rhetorical importance of the last two lines: F4/most modern texts set a more grammatical comma

Whiles we Gods wrathfull agent doe correct
Their proud contempt that beats his peace to heaven.

Philip of France as
France [1]

Peace be to England; if that warre returne
From France to England, there to live in peace:
England we love, and for that Englands sake,
With burden of our armor heere we sweat:
This toyle of ours should be a worke of thine;
But thou from loving England art so farre,
That thou hast under-wrought his lawfull King,
Cut off the sequence of posterity,
Out-faced Infant State, and done a rape
Upon the maiden vertue of the Crowne:
Looke heere upon thy brother Geffreyes face,
These eyes, these browes, were moulded out of his;
This little abstract doth containe that large,
Which died in Geffrey: and the hand of time,
Shall draw this breefe into as huge a volume:
That Geffrey was thy elder brother borne,
And this his sonne, England was Geffreys right,
And this is Geffreyes in the name of God: [2]
How comes it then that thou art call'd a King,
When living blood doth in these temples beat
Which owe the crowne, that thou ore-masterest?

King John

From whom hast thou this great commission France,[†]
To draw my answer from thy Articles?

France

Frō [3] that supernal Judge that stirs good thoughts
In any beast [4] of strong authoritie,
To looke into the blots and staines of right,
That Judge hath made me guardian to this boy,
Under whose warrant I impeach thy wrong,
And by whose helpe I meane to chastise it.   L4 - c

King John

Alack thou dost usurpe authoritie.

France

Excuse it is to beat usurping downe.

90
95
100
105
110
115

[P1] now King John has entered, the Ff prefix for King Philip becomes the title of his country, 'France', a very useful indicator of how he may want himself to behave and be perceived

[PCT2] at least one modern text starts a new sentence with the phrase 'in the name of God'; this has two deleterious effects; it removes the religious element of the argument that King Philip (presented as a devout man throughout the play) uses, and it replaces the dignity of the end of the speech with an element of anger, even petulance

[W3] F2/most modern texts = 'From', F1 = 'Frō , probably because of lack of column width

[W4] F2/most modern texts = 'breast', F1 = 'beast'

120	Eleanor as **Queen** [1]	Who is it thou dost call usurper France?
	Constance	Let me make answer : thy usurping sonne.
	Queen	Out insolent, thy bastard shall be King, That thou maist be a Queen, and checke the world.
125	**Constance**	My bed was ever to thy sonne as true As thine was to thy husband, and this boy Liker in feature to his father Geffrey Then thou and John, [2] in manners being as like, As raine to water, or devill to his damme ; My boy a bastard? by my soule I thinke
130		His father never was so true begot, It cannot be, and if thou wert his mother.
	Queen	Theres a good mother boy, that blots thy father† [3]

	Constance	There's a good grandame [4] boy →[5] That would blot thee.
135	**Austria**	Peace.
	Bastard	Heare the Cryer.
	Austria	What the devill art thou?

	Bastard	One that wil play the devill sir with you, And a may catch your hide and you alone : You are the Hare of whom the Proverb goes Whose valour plucks dead Lyons by the beard ; Ile smoake your skin-coat and I catch you right, Sirra looke too't, yfaith I will, yfaith.
140		
	Blanche	O well did he become that Lyons robe,
145		That did disrobe the Lion of that robe.

R4-c : 2. 1. 120 - 142

P [1] this is the first of several prefix changes for King John's mother, Eleanor: here, the prefix 'Queen' is a splendid indicator as to how she now presents herself

PCT [2] the Ff comma suggests Constance is pointing out that in both features and manners Arthur is akin to his father: some modern texts move the comma to after 'manners', essentially turning a debating point into an insult

PCT [3] probably because of lack of column width, F1 sets no punctuation (perhaps suggesting Eleanor interrupts her): F2/most modern texts set a period

W [4] Ff = 'grandame', which most modern texts set as 'grandam'

SP/LS [5] arguing there was insufficient width in the F1 column to set Ff's two short lines (6/4 syllables) as one, most modern texts join the two lines together, and then set the next three short lines (1/3 or 4/5 or 6) as a second single verse line: however, two pauses can be offered another way, viz. a hesitation after the first line before Constance's public statement of what Eleanor is trying to do; and after the fourth line, allowing the Bastard's unruly and undiplomatic comment full weight before Austria's (startled?) reply

15

	Bastard	It lies as sightly on the backe of him
		As great Alcides shooes upon an Asse :
		But Asse, Ile take that burthen from your backe,
		Or lay on that shall make your shoulders cracke.
150	**Austria**	What cracker is this same that deafes our eares
		With this abundance of superfluous breath?
		King Lewis,[1] determine what we shall doe strait.
	Lewis [2]	Women & fooles, breake off your conference.
		King John, this is the very summe of all :
155		England and Ireland, Angiers,[3] Toraine, Maine,
		In right of Arthur doe I claime of thee :
		Wilt thou resigne them, and lay downe thy Armes?

King John as
John [4]

My life as soone :   I doe defie thee France,
Arthur of Britaine, yeeld thee to my hand,
160 And out of my deare love Ile give thee more,
Then ere the coward hand of France can win ;
Submit thee boy.

Queen   Come to thy grandame child. }

Constance   Doe childe, goe to yt grandame childe,
165 Give grandame kingdome, and it grandame will
Give yt a plum, a cherry, and a figge,
There's a good grandame. }

Arthur   Good my mother peace,
I would that I were low laid in my grave,
170 I am not worth this coyle that's made for me.

Eleanor as
Queen Mother [5]   His mother shames him so, poore boy hee weepes.

---

[1] with the already seen confusion between the names of Lewis (the Dolphin) and Philip (the King), most modern texts consider Ff's setting of 'King Lewis' here a mistake and set 'King Philip' instead: however, Austria could be appealing to both men, as the addition of a simple comma between the two names 'King, Lewis' would show

[2] Ff set this speech for the (impatient?) Dolphin, a very undiplomatic comment and demand: most modern texts reassign the speech to King Philip

N/W [3] Ff = 'Angiers' which is in fact the capital of Anjou, the district claimed earlier on Arthur's behalf (line 12, page 1): thus most modern texts set 'Anjou'

[4] now the public posturing is over, and King John is directly challenged for the first time in the play, his prefix changes from one of status ('King John') to one of personal identity ('John')

[5] again Eleanor's Ff prefix shifts, from Queen to Qu{een} Mo{ther}, perhaps an indication as to how she may be trying to present herself to Arthur

Constance	Now shame upon you where she does or no,
	His grandames wrongs, and not his mothers shames
	Drawes [1] those heaven-moving pearles frō [2] his poor eies,
175	Which heaven shall take in nature of a fee:
	I, with these Christall beads heaven shall be brib'd
	To doe him Justice, and revenge on you.
Eleanor as **Queen** [3]	Thou monstrous slanderer of heaven and earth.
Constance	Thou monstrous Injurer of heaven and earth,
180	Call not me slanderer, thou and thine usurpe
	The Dominations, Royalties, and rights
	Of this oppressed boy; this is thy eldest sonnes sonne,
	Infortunate in nothing but in thee:
	Thy sinnes are visited in this poore childe,
185	The Canon of the Law is laide on him,
	Being but the second generation
	Removed from thy sinne-conceiving wombe.
John	Bedlam have done.
Constance	I have but this to say,
190	That he is not onely plagued for her sin,
	But God hath made her sinne and her, the plague
	On this removed issue, plagued for her,
	And with her plague her sinne: his injury
	Her injurie the Beadle to her sinne,
195	All punish'd in the person of this childe,
	And all for her, a plague upon her.
Queen	Thou unadvised scold, I can produce
	A Will, that barres the title of thy sonne.
Constance	I who doubts that, a Will: a wicked will,
200	A womans will, a cankred Grandams will.
France	Peace Lady, pause, or be more temperate,
	It ill beseemes this presence to cry ayme
	To these ill-tuned repetitions:
	Some Trumpet summon hither to the walles
205	These men of Angiers, let us heare them speake,
	Whose title they admit, Arthurs or Johns.

R4 - c

R4-c/L5-b : 2.1.167-200

[W] [1] Ff = 'Drawes', some modern texts = 'Draw'

[AB] [2] F2/most modern texts = 'from': probably because of lack of column width, F1 = 'frō'

[P] [3] as she attacks Constance Eleanor's Ff prefix shifts once more, from the nurturing 'Queen Mother' back to the (presumably) more status demanding 'Queen'

17

TRUMPET SOUNDS
ENTER A CITIZEN [1] UPON THE WALLES

Citizen	Who is it that hath warn'd us to the walles?
France	'Tis France, for England.
John	England for it selfe: } You men of Angiers, and my loving subjects.
France	You loving men of Angiers, Arthurs subjects, Our Trumpet call'd you to this gentle parle.
John	For our [2] advantage, therefore heare us first: These flagges of France that are advanced heere Before the eye and prospect of your Towne, Have hither march'd to your endamagement.

210

215

The Canons have their bowels full of wrath,
And ready mounted are they to spit forth
Their Iron indignation 'gainst your walles:
220   All preparation for a bloody siedge
And merciles proceeding, by these French.

Comfort [3] yours [4] Citties eies, your winking gates:
And but for our approch, those sleeping stones,
That as a waste doth girdle you about
225   By the compulsion of their Ordinance,
By this time from their fixed beds of lime
Had bin dishabited, and wide havocke made
For bloody power to rush uppon your peace.

But on the sight of us your lawfull King,
230   Who painefully with much expedient march
Have brought a counter-checke before your gates,
To save unscratch'd your Citties threatned cheekes:
Behold the French amaz'd vouchsafe a parle,
And now insteed [5] of bulletts wrapt in fire
235   To make a shaking fever in your walles,

SD/N [1] most modern texts add extra Citizens to the entry: also, many modern texts suggest the 'Citizen' and 'Hubert', whom Ff introduce later in this scene (page 22), are one and the same character and combine them accordingly under the prefix 'Hubert': see *The Arden Shakespeare King John*, op. cit., page 191 - 2 and the specific Introduction to this play for further details: this text will follow Ff and present two different characters

W [2] Ff/most modern texts = 'our', one gloss = 'your'

W [3] even though commentators accept Ff's reading as making sense (especially in an ironic vein), some modern texts remove the period at the end of the previous line and alter F3 - 4's 'Comfort your' to 'Confront your'

W [4] F3 - 4/most modern texts = 'your', F1 - 2 = 'yours'

W [5] F1 - 2 = 'insteed', F3/most modern texts = 'instead', F4 = 'in stead'

They shoote but calme words, folded up in smoake,
To make a faithlesse errour in your eares,
Which trust accordingly kinde Cittizens,
And let us in. [1]

240   Your King, whose labour'd spirits
Fore-wearied in this action of swift speede,
Craves harbourage within your Citie walles.

France   When I have saide, make answer to us both.

Loe in this right hand, whose protection
245   Is most divinely vow'd upon the right
Of him it holds, stands yong Plantagenet,
Sonne to the elder brother of this man,   L5 - b
And King ore him, and all that he enjoyes :
For this downe-troden equity, we tread
250   In warlike march, these greenes before your Towne,
Being no further enemy to you
Then the constraint of hospitable zeale,
In the releefe of this oppressed childe,
Religiously provokes.
255   Be pleased then
To pay that dutie which you truly owe,
To him that owes it, namely, this yong Prince,
And then our Armes, like to a muzled Beare,
Save in aspect, hath all offence seal'd up :
260   Our Cannons malice vainly shall be spent
Against th'involverable [2] clouds of heaven,
And with a blessed and un-vext retyre,
With unhack'd swords, and Helmets all unbruis'd,
We will beare home that lustie blood againe,
265   Which heere we came to spout against your Towne,
And leave your children, wives, and you in peace.

But if you fondly passe our proffer'd offer,
'Tis not the rounder [3] of your old-fac'd walles,
Can hide you from our messengers of Warre,
270   Though all these English, and their discipline
Were harbour'd in their rude circumference :
Then tell us, Shall your Citie call us Lord,
In that behalfe which we have challeng'd it?

L5 - b / R5 - b : 2. 1. 229 - 264

PCT [1] Ff set a period, and rhetorically a final sentence to end the speech makes enormous sense and could have
  great emotional/debating impact on all who hear: most modern texts reduce the impact by replacing the period with
  either a comma or a dash, allowing the speech to continue without its original final flourish

W [2] F2/most modern texts = 'invulnerable', F1 = 'involverable'

W [3] Ff = 'rounder', most modern texts = 'roundure'

		Or shall we give the signall to our rage,
275		And stalke in blood to our possession?
	Citizen	In breefe, we are the King of Englands subjects [1]
		For him, and in his right, we hold this Towne.
	John	Acknowledge then the King, and let me in.
	Citizen	That can we not: but he that proves the King
280		To him will we prove loyall, till that time
		Have we ramm'd up our gates against the world.
	John	Doth not the Crowne of England, proove the
		King?
		And if not that, I bring you Witnesses
285		Twice fifteene thousand hearts of Englands breed.
	Bastard	Bastards and else.
	John	To verifie our title with their lives.
	France	As many and as well-borne bloods as those.
	Bastard	Some Bastards too.
290	**France**	Stand in his face to contradict his claime.
	Citizen	Till you compound whose right is worthiest,
		We for the worthiest hold the right from both.
	John	Then God forgive the sinne of all those soules,
		That to their everlasting residence,
295		Before the dew of evening fall, shall fleete
		In dreadfull triall of our kingdomes King.
	France	Amen, Amen, mount Chevaliers to Armes.

	Bastard	Saint George that swindg'd the Dragon,
		And ere since° sit's on's horsebacke at mine Hostesse dore° [2]
300		Teach us some fence.
		[3] Sirrah, were I at home
		At your den sirrah, with your Lionnesse,
		I would set an Oxe-head to your Lyons hide:
		And make a monster of you.

[PCT] [1] F2/most modern texts set a comma, allowing time for a reasoned reply: F1 sets no punctuation as if the Citizen is not quite as confident as F2 would suggest

[LS/W] [2] Ff set two irregular lines(7/12 syllables) suggesting there may be a slight pause before the Bastard starts speaking, which could well cover the movement of the forces readying themselves for battle: most modern texts set two regular lines by restructuring as shown and by expanding Ff's 'on's' in the second line to 'on his'

[WHO] [3] most modern texts suggest this is spoken to Austria

05	Austria	Peace, no more.

Bastard   O tremble: for you heare the Lyon rore.

John   Up higher to the plaine, where we'l set forth
In best appointment all our Regiments.

Bastard   Speed then to take advantage of the field.

10   **France**   It shall be so, and at the other hill
Command the rest to stand, God and our right,[1]

[Exeunt] [2]

**HEERE AFTER EXCURSIONS, ENTER THE HERALD OF FRANCE
WITH TRUMPETS TO THE GATES**

French Herald   You men of Angiers open wide your gates,   R 5 - b
And let yong Arthur Duke of Britaine in,
Who by the hand of France, this day hath made
15   Much worke for teares in many an English mother,
Whose sonnes lye scattered on the bleeding ground:
Many a widdowes husband groveling lies,
Coldly embracing the discoloured earth,[†3]
And victorie with little losse doth play
20   Upon the dancing banners of the French,
Who are at hand triumphantly displayed
To enter Conquerors, and to proclaime
Arthur of Britaine, Englands King, and yours.

ENTER ENGLISH HERALD WITH TRUMPET

English Herald   Rejoyce you men of Angiers, ring your bels,
25   King John, your king and Englands, doth approach,
Commander of this hot malicious day,
Their Armours that march'd hence so silver bright,
Hither returne all gilt with Frenchmens blood:
There stucke no plume in any English Crest,
30   That is removed by a staffe of France. [4]

Our colours do returne in those same hands
That did display them when we first marcht forth:

R 5 - b / L 66 - b   :   2. 1. 293 - 320

[PCT 1]   F1 sets a comma, perhaps suggesting the final remark tails off as every one leaves the stage: F2/most modern
texts set a period
[SD 2]   most modern texts suggest it is just the battle groups who exit, while the Citizens stay aloft and watch
[W 3]   Ff/most modern texts = 'earth', F1 = 'earrh'
[PCT 4]   Ff set a period, suggesting the final statement is to be treated as a deliberate increase of intensity in the
rhetorical bragging process: most modern texts reduce this to some form of major punctuation

		And like a jolly troope of Huntsmen come
		Our lustie English, all with purpled hands,
335		Dide in the dying slaughter of their foes,
		Open your gates, and give the Victors way.

Hubert [1] Heralds, from off our towres we might behold
From first to last, the on-set and retyre,
Of both your[2] Armies, whose equality
340 By our best eyes cannot be censured :
Blood hath bought blood, and blowes have answerd blowes : †
Strength matcht with strength, and power confronted
  power,
Both are alike, and both alike we like :
345 One must prove greatest.
                    While they weigh so even,
We hold our Towne for neither : yet for both.

**ENTER THE TWO KINGS WITH THEIR POWERS,
AT SEVERALL DOORES**

John France, hast thou yet more blood to cast away?

Say, shall the currant of our right rome [3] on,
350 Whose passage vext with thy impediment,
Shall leave his native channell, and ore-swell
⁴ with course disturb'd even thy confining shores,
Unlesse thou let his silver Water, keepe
A peacefull progresse to the Ocean.

355 **France** England thou hast not sav'd one drop of blood
In this hot triall more then we of France,
Rather lost more.
              And by this hand I sweare
That swayes the earth this Climate over-lookes,
360 Before we will lay downe our just-borne Armes,
Wee'l put thee downe, 'gainst whom these Armes wee beare,†
Or adde a royall number to the dead :
Gracing the scroule that tels of this warres losse,
With slaughter coupled to the name of kings.

N/P [1] Ff introduce the character of Hubert for the first time: those few modern texts who separate the characters of Hubert and the Citizen usually do not follow Ff here, and assign this and all the subsequent Ff Hubert speeches to the Citizen instead (not introducing Hubert until the scene they term Act Three Scene 3, page 44 this script)

W [2] F1 = 'yonr', F2/most modern texts = 'your'

W [3] F2 = 'runne', F1 = 'rome', which most modern texts set as 'roam'

VP [4] F2/most modern texts set the verse indicator of a capital letter to start, viz. 'With', F1 seems to set the line as prose via a lower case 'with'

365	**Bastard**	Ha Majesty: how high thy glory towres,
		When the rich blood of kings is set on fire:
		Oh now doth death line his dead chaps with steele,
		The swords of souldiers are his teeth, his phangs,
		And now he feasts, mousing the flesh of men
370		In undetermin'd differences of kings.

Why stand these royall fronts amazed thus:
Cry havocke kings, backe to the stained field
You equall Potents, fierie kindled spirits,
Then let confusion of one part confirm
The others peace: till then, blowes, blood, and death.

	John	Whose party do the Townesmen yet admit?	L6 - b
	France	Speake Citizens for England, whose [1] your king.	
	Hubert	The king of England, when we know the king.	
	France	Know him in us, that heere hold up his right.	
380	**John**	In Us, that are our owne great Deputie,	
		And beare possession of our Person heere,	
		Lord of our presence Angiers, and of you.	

	France	A greater powre then We denies all this,
		And till it be undoubted, we do locke
385		Our former scruple in our strong barr'd gates:
		Kings of our feare, [2] untill our feares resolv'd
		Be by some certaine king, purg'd and depos'd.

	Bastard	By heaven, these scroyles of Angiers flout you kings,[†]
		And stand securely on their battelments,
390		As in a Theater, whence they gape and point
		At your industrious Scenes and acts of death.

Your Royall presences be rul'd by mee,
Do like the Mutines of Jerusalem,
Be friends a-while, and both conjoyntly bend
Your sharpest Deeds of malice on this Towne.

By East and West let France and England mount
Their battering Canon charged to the mouthes,
Till their soule-fearing clamours have braul'd downe
The flintie ribbes of this contemptuous Citie,

[1] F1 = 'whose', F2/most modern texts = 'who's'

[2] Ff/some modern texts = 'Kings of our feare': one interesting modern gloss = 'Kings are our fears', while one text sets the rather obscure 'King'd of our fears,'

400		I'de play incessantly upon these Jades,
		Even till unfenced desolation
		Leave them as naked as the vulgar ayre :
		That done, dissever your united strengths,
		And part your mingled colours once againe,
405		Turne face to face, and bloody point to point :
		Then in a moment Fortune shall cull forth
		Out of one side her happy Minion,
		To whom in favour she shall give the day,
		And kisse him with a glorious victory :
410		How like you this wilde counsell mighty States,
		Smackes it not something of the policie.
	John	Now by the sky that hangs above our heads,
		I like it well.
		France, shall we knit our powres,
415		And lay this Angiers even with the ground,
		Then after fight who shall be king of it?
	Bastard	And if thou hast the mettle of a king,
		Being wrong'd as we are by this peevish Towne : †1
		Turne thou the mouth of thy Artillerie,
420		As we will ours, against these sawcie walles,
		And when that we have dash'd them to the ground,
		Why then defie each other, and pell-mell,
		Make worke upon our selves, for heaven or hell.
	France	Let it be so : say, where will you assault?
425	**John**	We from the West will send destruction
		Into this Cities bosome.
	Austria	I from the North.
	France	Our Thunder from the South, ²
		Shall raine their drift of bullets on this Towne.
430	**Bastard**	³ O prudent discipline!
		From North to South :
		Austria and France shoot in each others mouth.
		Ile stirre them to it : Come, away, away.

W 1   F1 = 'Townc', F2/most modern texts = 'Towne'

LS 2   the actor has choice as to which two of these three short lines may be joined as one line of split verse

A 3   some modern texts suggest this is spoken as an aside, though once again the Bastard's sense of plain-speaking irreverence makes it equally likely he speaks this aloud

24

Hubert	Heare us great kings, vouchsafe awhile to stay
435	And I shall shew you peace, and faire-fac'd league:
	Win you this Citie without stroke, or wound,
	Rescue those breathing lives to dye in beds,
	That heere come sacrifices for the field.
	Persever not, but heare me mighty kings.
440 **John**	Speake on with favour, we are bent to heare.
Hubert	That daughter there of Spaine, the Lady Blanch
	Is neere [1] to England, looke upon the yeeres
	Of Lewes the Dolphin,[2] and that lovely maid.

If lustie love should go in quest of beautie,   R6 - b
445   Where should he finde it fairer, then in Blanch:
        If zealous love should go in search of vertue,
        Where should he finde it purer then in Blanch?

        If love ambitious, sought a match of birth,
        Whose veines bound richer blood then Lady Blanch?

450   Such as she is, in beautie, vertue, birth,
        Is the yong Dolphin every way compleat,
        If not compleat of,[3] say he is not shee,
        And she againe wants nothing, to name want,
        If want it be not, that she is not hee:
455   He is the halfe part of a blessed man,
        Left to be finished by such as shee,
        And she a faire divided excellence,
        Whose fulnesse of perfection lyes in him.

        O two such silver currents when they joyne
460   Do glorifie the bankes that bound them in:
        And two such shores, to two such streames made one,
        Two such controlling bounds shall you be, kings,
        To these two Princes, if you marrie them:
        This Union shall do more then batterie can
465   To our fast closed gates: for at this match,
        With swifter spleene then powder can enforce
        The mouth of passage shall we fling wide ope,
        And give you entrance: but without this match,
        The sea enraged is not halfe so deafe,
470   Lyons more confident, Mountaines and rockes

R6 - b / L7 - b : 2. 1. 416 - 452

[W][1] Ff = 'neere', some modern texts set 'niece'

[N/W][2] within the dialogue, Ff set 'Dolphin/Daulphin' throughout, which most modern texts set as the more currently recogniseable 'Dauphin': this is the only time this will be footnoted in this text

[W][3] Ff/most modern texts = 'compleate of', for clarity one gloss = 'completed'

25

	More free from motion,[†1] no not death himselfe
	In mortall furie halfe so peremptorie,
	As we to keepe this Citie.
	}
Bastard	Heeres a stay,
475	That shakes the rotten carkasse of old death
	Out of his ragges.
	Here's a large mouth indeede,
	That spits forth death, and mountaines, rockes, and seas,
	Talkes as familiarly of roaring Lyons,
480	As maids of thirteene do of puppi-dogges.
	What Cannoneere begot this lustie blood,
	He speakes plaine Cannon fire,[2] and smoake, and bounce,
	He gives the bastinado with his tongue:
	Our eares are cudgel'd, not a word of his
485	But buffets better then a fist of France:
	Zounds, I was never so bethumpt with words,
	Since I first cal'd my brothers father Dad.
Eleanor as **Old Queen**[3]	Son, list to this conjunction, make this match [4]
	Give with our Neece a dowrie large enough,
490	For by this knot, thou shalt so surely tye
	Thy now unsur'd [†5] assurance to the Crowne,
	That yon greene boy shall have no Sunne to ripe
	The bloome that promiseth a mightie fruite.
	I see a yeelding in the lookes of France:
495	Marke how they whisper, urge them while their soules
	Are capeable of this ambition,
	Least zeale now melted by the windie breath
	Of soft petitions, pittie and remorse,
	Coole and congeale againe to what it was.
500 **Hubert**	Why answer not the double Majesties,
	This friendly treatie of our threatned Towne.

[W1] F2/most modern texts = 'from motion', F1 = 'ftom morion' (with the middle consonant of 'morion' blurred)

[W2] Ff set two separate words 'Cannon fire' which some modern texts set as a compound epithet, viz. 'cannon-fire', or add a comma to part the words, 'cannon, fire'

[P3] as Eleanor adopts the role of advisor, so her prefix changes to 'Old Qu.{een}), again an indication of how she might be handling the moment, and an important reminder of how John regards her, thus enhancing his sense of loss when told of her death later in the play

[PCT4] probably because of lack of column width F1 shows no punctuation: if this were to stand, it might suggest in the urgency of the situation Eleanor is moving swiftly from one idea to the next: F2/most modern texts set a comma

[W5] F1 = 'unsur d', F2/most modern texts = 'unsur'd'

France	Speake England first, that hath bin forward first
	To speake unto this Cittie: what say you?

John
505 If that the Dolphin there thy Princely sonne,
Can in this booke of beautie read, I love:
Her Dowrie shall weigh equall with a Queene:
For Angiers,[1] and faire Toraine[2] Maine, Poyctiers,
And all that we upon this side[†3] the Sea,
(Except this Cittie now by us besiedg'd)
510 Finde liable to our Crowne and Dignitie,
Shall gild her bridall bed and make her rich   L7 - b
In titles, honors, and promotions,
As she in beautie, education, blood,
Holdes hand with any Princesse of the world.

515 **France** What sai'st thou boy? looke in the Ladies face.

Lewis as Dolphin[4]
I do my Lord, and in her eie I find
A wonder, or a wondrous miracle,
The shadow of my selfe form'd in her eye,
Which being but the shadow of your sonne,
520 Becomes a sonne[5] and makes your sonne a shadow:
I do protest I never lov'd my selfe
Till now, infixed I beheld my selfe,
Drawne in the flattering table of her eie.

[Whispers with Blanch]

Bastard Drawne in the flattering table of her eie,
525 Hang'd in the frowning wrinkle of her brow,
And quarter'd in her heart, hee doth espie
Himselfe loves traytor, this is pittie now;
That hang'd, and drawne, and quarter'd there should be
In such a love, so vile a Lout as he.

530 **Blanche** My unckles will in this respect is mine,
If he see ought in you that makes him like,
That anything he see's which moves his liking,
I can with ease translate it to my will:
Or if you will, to speake more properly,
535 I will enforce it easlie to my love.

[N1] as earlier (footnote 3, page 16) Ff set the name of the town, 'Angiers', most modern texts set the district 'Anjou'

[PCT2] to separate the names most modern texts add F2's comma, F1 sets no punctuation

[W3] F1 = 'fide', F2/most modern texts = 'side'

[P4] faced with what is an obviously political match, it is fascinating to note that his personal prefix 'Lewis', which has been used until now, is replaced by the prefix of status 'Dolphin': most modern texts do not set the change

[W5] Ff = 'sonne', which for clarity most modern texts set as 'sun' (the pun will be heard no matter what the spelling)

Further I will not flatter you, my Lord,
That all I see in you is worthie love,
Then this, that nothing do I see in you,
Though churlish thoughts themselves should bee your
540   Judge,
That I can finde, should merit any hate.

John   What saie these yong-ones?
                                 What say you my
Neece?

545 **Blanche**   That she is bound in honor still to do
What you in wisedome still [1] vouchsafe to say.

John   Speake then Prince Dolphin, can you love this
Ladie?

Dolphin   Nay aske me if I can refraine from love,
550   For I doe love her most unfainedly.

John   Then do I give Volquessen, Toraine, Maine,
Poyctiers and Anjow, these five Provinces
With her to thee, and this addition more,
Full thirty thousand Markes of English coyne :
555   Phillip of France, if thou be pleas'd withall,
Command thy sonne and daughter[†2] to joyne hands.

France   It likes us well young Princes :[3] close your hands [4]

Austria And your lippes too, for I am well assur'd,
That I did so when I was first assur'd. [5]

560 **France**   Now Cittizens of Angires ope your gates,
Let in that amitie which you have made,
For at Saint Maries Chappell presently,
The rights [6] of marriage shall be solemniz'd.

Is not the Ladie Constance in this troope?
565   I know she is not for this match made up,
Her presence would have interrupted much.

Where is she and her sonne, tell me, who knowes?

[W1] Ff/most modern texts = 'still', glosses include 'shall' and 'will'

[W2] F2/most modern texts = 'daughter', F1 = 'daughtet'

[PCT3] the Ff punctuation establishes a peremptory summation to the fate of the 'young Princes': some modern texts set the more seemingly courteous 'It likes us well. Young princes, close your hands.'

[PCT4] F1 sets no punctuation as if Austria interrupts him: F2/most modern texts set a period

[SD5] some modern texts suggest Blanche and Lewis join hands (sometimes adding that they kiss)

[W6] F1 - 3 = 'rights' suggesting a commercial element to the marriage: F4/most modern texts set 'rites'

Dolphin	She is sad and passionate at your highnes Tent.
France	And by my faith, this league that we have made
570	Will give her sadnesse very little cure:
	Brother of England, how may we content
	This widdow Lady?
	In her right we came,
	Which we God knowes, have turn d [1] another way,
575	To our owne vantage.
John	We will heale up all, }
	For wee'l create yong Arthur Duke of Britaine
	And Earle of Richmond, and this rich faire Towne
	We make him Lord of.
580	Call the Lady Constance,
	Some speedy Messenger bid her repaire
	To our solemnity: I trust we shall,
	(If not fill up the measure of her will)
	Yet in some measure satisfie her so,
585	That we shall stop her exclamation,
	Go we as well as hast will suffer us,
	To this unlook'd for unprepared pompe.

R7 - b

[Exeunt]

Bastard	Mad world, mad kings, mad composition:
	John to stop Arthurs Title in the whole,
590	Hath willingly departed with a part,
	And France, whose armour Conscience buckled on,
	Whom zeale and charitie brought to the field,
	As Gods owne souldier, rounded in the eare,
	With that same purpose-changer, that slye divel,
595	That Broker, that still breakes the pate of faith,
	That dayly breake-vow, he that winnes of all,

> [2] Of kings, of beggers, old men, yong men, maids,
> Who having no externall thing to loose,
> But the word Maid, cheats the poore Maide of that.

600	That smooth-fac'd Gentleman, tickling commoditie,
	Commoditie, the byas of the world,
	The world, who of it selfe is peysed well,
	Made to run even, upon even ground;

R7 - b / L8 - b : 2. 1. 544 - 576

[W][1] F2/most modern texts = 'turned', F1 = 'turn d'

[PCT][2] most modern texts suggest these three lines are a side line to the major line of thought, and mark them off with either dashes or brackets, removing Ff's period at the end of the third line: however, this ungrammatical Ff period seems to suggest the Bastard needs a fresh start to his thinking process as he begins to realise just how all-encompassing 'commoditie' really is

Till this advantage, this vile drawing byas,
505   This sway of motion, this commoditie,
Makes it take head from all indifferency,
From all direction, purpose, course, intent.

And this same byas, this Commoditie,
This Bawd, this Broker,this all-changing-word,
510   Clap'd on the outward eye of fickle France,
Hath drawne him from his owne determin'd ayd,
From a resolv'd and honourable warre,
To a most base and vile-concluded peace.

And why rayle I on this Commoditie?

515   But for because he hath not wooed me yet :
Not that I have the power to clutch my hand,
When his faire Angels would salute my palme,
But for my hand, as unattempted yet,
Like a poore begger, raileth on the rich.

520   Well, whiles I am a begger, I will raile,
And say there is no sin but to be rich :
And being rich, my vertue then shall be,
To say there is no vice, but beggerie :
Since Kings breake faith upon commoditie,
525   Gaine be my Lord, for I will worship thee.

[Exit]

Actus Secundus [1]

ENTER CONSTANCE, ARTHUR, AND SALISBURY

Constance	Gone to be married?

         Gone to sweare a peace?

False blood to false blood joyn'd.

         Gone to be friends?

5   Shall Lewis have Blaunch, and Blaunch [2] those Provinces?

It is not so, thou hast mispoke, misheard,
Be well advis'd, tell ore thy tale againe.

It cannot be, thou do'st but say 'tis so.

I trust I may not trust thee, for thy word
10   Is but the vaine breath of a common man :
Beleeve me, I doe not beleeve thee man,
I have a Kings oath to the contrarie.

Thou shalt be punish'd for thus frighting me,
For I am sicke, and capeable of feares,   L8 - b
15   Opprest with wrongs, and therefore full of feares,
A widdow, husbandles, subject to feares,
A woman naturally borne [3] to feares ;
And though thou now confesse thou didst but jest
With my vext spirits, I cannot take a Truce,
20   But they will quake and tremble all this day.

What dost thou meane by shaking of thy head?

Why dost thou looke so sadly on my sonne?

What meanes that hand upon that breast of thine?

Why holdes thine eie that lamentable rhewme,
25   Like a proud river peering ore his bounds?

L8 - b / R8 - b : 3. 1. 1 - 23

[ALT 1] most modern texts name this Act Three, Ff term it Act Two

[W 2] though the same Compositor (B) set 'Blanche' earlier in the play, here both times the name is spelled as 'Blaunch' , which most texts regularise to 'Blanche': the difference in spelling is possibly due to personal preferences of the two scribes some commentators presume to have prepared the manuscript copy for the Playhouse text: however, if the F1 spelling is authorial it could delineate a wonderful dismissal by Constance of Blanche's character as somewhat insipid (viz. emphasising the French for 'white', 'blaunche')

[W 3] F3/most modern texts = 'born', viz. her fears come about from her being born a woman, F1 - 2 = 'borne', i.e. her recent experiences as a woman have brought her ('carried' her) to her fears

Be these sad signes confirmers of thy words?

Then speake againe, not all thy former tale,
But this one word, whether thy tale be true.

Salisbury
As true as I beleeve you thinke them false,
30   That give you cause to prove my saying true.

Constance
Oh if thou teach me to beleeve this sorrow,
Teach thou this sorrow, how to make me dye,
And let beleefe, and life encounter so,
As doth the furie of two desperate men,
35   Which in the very meeting fall, and dye.

Lewes marry Blaunch?
                O boy, then where art thou?

France friend with England, what becomes of me?

Fellow be gone: I cannot brooke thy sight,
40   This newes hath made thee a most ugly man.

Salisbury
What other harme have I good Lady done,
But spoke the harme, that is by others done?

Constance
Which harme within it selfe so heynous is,
As it makes harmefull all that speake of it.

45 **Arthur**
I do beseech you Madam be content.

Constance
If thou that bidst me be content, wert grim
Ugly, and slandrous to thy Mothers wombe,
Full of unpleasing blots, and sightlesse staines,
Lame, foolish, crooked, swart, prodigious,
50   Patch'd with foule Moles, and eye-offending markes,
I would not care, I then would be content,
For then I should not love thee: no, nor thou
Become thy great birth, nor deserve a Crowne.

But thou art faire, and at thy birth (deere boy)
55   Nature and Fortune joyn'd to make thee great.

Of Natures guifts, thou mayst with Lillies boast,
And with the halfe-blowne Rose.
                   But Fortune, oh,
She is corrupted, chang'd, and wonne from thee,
Sh'adulterates hourely with thine Unckle John,
60   And with her golden hand hath pluckt on France
To tread downe faire respect of Soveraigntie,
And made his Majestie the bawd to theirs.

		France is a Bawd to Fortune, and king John,
65		That strumpet Fortune, that usurping John :
		Tell me thou fellow, is not France forsworne?

Envenom[†1] him with words, or get thee gone,
And leave those woes alone, which I alone
Am bound to under-beare.
}

Salisbury (70)
Pardon me Madam,
I may not goe without you to the kings.

Constance
Thou maist, thou shalt, I will not go with thee,
I will instruct my sorrowes to bee proud,
For greefe is proud, and makes his owner stoope,[2]
To me and to the state of my great greefe,
Let kings assemble :   for my greefe's so great,
That no supporter but the huge firme earth
Can hold it up :   [3] here I and sorrowes sit,
Heere is my Throne, bid kings come bow to it. [4]

R8 - b

(marginal line numbers: 70, 75)

[W 1] F2/most modern texts = 'Envenom', F1 = 'Euvenom'

[PCT 2] Ff set a comma, suggesting a whirling mind, running thoughts together: some modern texts set a period, making her act of defiance somewhat more rational

[SD 3] most modern texts suggest Constance now sits on the floor

[SD 4] some modern texts suggest Salisbury now exits: however, since most of them do not follow Ff and set the next scene as the start of a new Act, but simply bring on the various dignitaries as a continuation of the current scene, there seems no reason for Salisbury to exit before they arrive

Actus Tertius, Scœna prima [1]

**ENTER KING JOHN, FRANCE, DOLPHIN, BLANCH, ELIANOR, PHILIP,
AUSTRIA, CONSTANCE [2]**

France	'Tis true (faire daughter) and this blessed day,
	Ever in France shall be kept festivall :
	To solemnize this day the glorious sunne
	Stayes in his course, and playes the Alchymist,
5	Turning with splendor of his precious eye
	The meager cloddy earth to glittering gold :
	The yearely course that brings this day about,
	Shall never see it, but a holy day. [3]
Constance	A wicked day, and not a holy day. [4]
10	What hath this day deserv'd? what hath it[†5] done,
	That it in golden letters should beset
	Among the high tides in the Kalender?
	Nay, rather turne this day out of the weeke,
	This day of shame, oppression, perjury.
15	Or if it must stand still, let wives with childe
	Pray that their burthens may not fall this day,
	Lest that their hopes prodigiously be crost :
	But (on this day) let Sea-men feare no wracke,
	No bargaines breake that are not this day made ;
20	This day all things begun, come to ill end,
	Yea, faith it selfe to hollow falshood change.
France	By heaven Lady, you shall have no cause
	To curse the faire proceedings of this day :
	Have I not pawn'd to you my Majesty?

L 9 - c : 3. 1. 75 - 98

SD/COMP [1] as the previous footnote mentions, most modern texts set the exit as a continuation of the previous scene, and set neither a new Act nor Scene: also, F1 does not follow its normal practice of setting a horizontal line to separate the Act/Scene designation from the first stage direction

SD [2] most modern texts add Attendants to the entry, and, since Constance according to most modern texts is already on-stage, they do not include her with the others

W [3] F1 - 3 = 'holy day', F4 = 'Holy-day', most modern texts = 'holiday'

SD [4] most modern texts suggest Constance now rises, though there is nothing in the dialogue to suggest now instead of a later point in the scene

W [5] F1 = 'ie', F2/most modern texts - 'it'

Constance	You have beguil'd me with a counterfeit
25	Resembling Majesty, which being touch'd and tride,
	Proves valuelesse : you are forsworne, forsworne,
	You came in Armes to spill mine enemies bloud,
	But now in Armes, you strengthen it with yours.
	The grapling vigor, and rough frowne of Warre
30	Is cold [1] in amitie, and painted peace,
	And our oppression hath made up this league :
	Arme, arme, you heavens, against these perjur'd Kings,
	A widdow cries, be husband to me (heavens) [2]
	Let not the howres of this ungodly day
35	Weare out the daies [3] in Peace ; but ere Sun-set,
	Set armed discord 'twixt these perjur'd Kings,
	Heare me, Oh, heare me.
Austria	Lady Constance, peace.
Constance	War, war, no peace, peace is to me a warre :
40	O Lymoges, O Austria, thou dost shame
	That bloudy spoyle : thou slave, thou wretch, ÿ [4] coward,
	Thou little valiant, great in villanie,
	Thou ever strong upon the stronger side ;
	Thou Fortunes Champion, that do'st never fight
45	But when her humourous Ladiship is by
	To teach thee safety : thou art perjur'd too,
	And sooth'st up greatnesse.
	What a foole art thou,
	A ramping foole, to brag, and stamp, and sweare,
50	Upon my partie : thou cold blooded slave,
	Hast thou not spoke like thunder on my side?
	Beene sworne my Souldier, bidding me depend
	Upon thy starres, thy fortune, and thy strength,
	And dost thou now fall over to my foes?
55	Thou weare a Lyons hide, doff it for shame,
	And hang a Calves skin on those recreant limbes.
Austria	O that a man should speake those words to me.

---

[1] Ff/most modern texts = 'cold', modern glosses include 'cool'd' and 'clad'

[2] Ff = '(heavens)' with no punctuation following , some modern texts = ', God!'

[3] Ff set the plural 'daies', some modern texts set the singular 'day'

[4] F1 = 'ÿ', (printed as such because of lack of column width), F2/most modern texts = 'thou'

•Philip • [1]	And hang a Calves-skin on those recreant limbs [2]	
Austria	Thou dar'st not say so villaine for thy life.	L9 - c
60 Philip	And hang a Calves-skin on those recreant limbs.	
John	We like not this, thou dost forget they selfe.	

ENTER PANDULPH

France	Heere comes the holy Legat of the Pope.
Pandulph	Haile you annointed deputies of heaven ; [3]
	To thee King John my holy errand is :
65	I Pandulph, of faire Millane Cardinall,
	And from Pope Innocent the Legate heere,
	Doe in his name religiously demand
	Why thou against the Church, our holy Mother,
	So wilfully dost spurne ; and force perforce
70	Keepe Stephen Langton chosen Arshbishop [4]
	Of Canterbury from that holy Sea : [5]
	This in our foresaid holy Fathers name
	Pope Innocent, I doe demand of thee.
John	What earthie name to Interrogatories
75	Can tast [6] the free breath of a sacred King?
	Thou canst not (Cardinall) devise a name
	So slight, unworthy, and ridiculous
	To charge me to an answere, as the Pope :
	Tell him this tale, and from the mouth of England,
80	Adde thus much more, that no Italian Priest
	Shall tythe or toll in our dominions :
	But as we, under heaven,[7] are supreame head,
	So under him that great supremacy
	Where we doe reigne, we will alone uphold
85	Without th'assistance of a mortall hand :
	So tell the Pope, all reverence set apart
	To him and his usurp'd authoritie.

[P]**1** as in this and the following speech the Bastard deliberately insults/challenges Austria by repeating Constance's dismissive words, Ff change his prefix from that of status ('Bastard') to the personal 'Philip', a splendid clue for the momentary change in character

PCT 2 F1 sets no punctuation, as if Austria interrupts him: F2/most modern texts set a period

3 Ff = 'heaven;', some modern texts = 'God!'

4 F1 - 2 = 'Arshbishop', F3/most modern texts = 'Archbishop'

5 F4/most modern texts = 'see', F1-3 = 'Sea'

6 Ff = 'tast', modern glosses include 'task' and 'tax'

7 Ff = 'heaven', some modern texts = 'God'

France	Brother of England, you blaspheme in this.
John	Though you, and all the Kings of Christendom
90		Are led so grossely by this medling Priest,
	Dreading the curse that money may buy out,
	And by the merit of vilde gold, drosse, dust,
	Purchase corrupted pardon of a man,
	Who in that sale sels pardon from himselfe :
95		Though you, and al the rest so grossely led,
	This jugling witchcraft with revennue cherish,
	Yet I alone, alone doe me oppose
	Against the Pope, and count his friends my foes.
Pandulph	Then by the lawfull power that I have,
100		Thou shalt stand curst, and excommunicate,
	And blessed shall he be that doth revolt
	From his Allegeance to an heretique,
	And meritorious shall that hand be call'd,
	Canonized and worship'd as a Saint,
105		That takes away by any secret course
	Thy hatefull life.
Constance	O lawfull let it be
	That I have roome with Rome to curse a while,
	Good Father Cardinall, cry thou Amen
110		To my keene curses ; for without my wrong
	There is no tongue hath power to curse him right.
Pandulph	There's Law and Warrant (Lady) for my curse.
Constance	And for mine too, when Law can do no right.
	Let it be lawfull, that Law barre no wrong :
115		Law cannot give my childe his kingdome heere ;
	For he that holds his Kingdome, holds the Law :
	Therefore since Law it selfe is perfect wrong,
	How can the Law forbid my tongue to curse?
Pandulph	Philip of France, on perill of a curse,
120		Let goe the hand of that Arch-heretique,
	And raise the power of France upon his head,
	Unlesse he doe submit himselfe to Rome.
'Eleanor'	Look'st thou pale France? do not let go thy hand.
Constance	Looke to that [1] Devill, lest that France repent,
125 | | And by disjoyning hands hell lose a soule. |

R9 - c

R 9 - c / L 10 - c : 3. 1. 161 - 197

PCT/W/WHO [1]
      for clarity most modern texts add a comma: some unnecessarily alter Ff's 'that' to 'it', and needlessly
suggest that Constance speaks just to John

	Austria	King Philip, listen to the Cardinall.
	Philip as **Bastard**	And hang a Calves-skin on his recreant limbs.
	Austria	Well ruffian, I must pocket up these wrongs, Because,[1]
130	**Bastard**	Your breeches best may carry them. ⎫
	John	Philip, what saist thou to the Cardinall?
	Constance	What should he say, but as the Cardinall?
	Dolphin	Bethinke you father, for the difference Is purchase of a heavy curse from Rome,
135		Or the light losse of England, for a friend: Forgoe the easier.
	Blanche	Thats[†2] the curse of Rome. ⎫
	Constance	O Lewis, stand fast, the devill tempts thee heere In likenesse of a new untrimmed Bride.
140	**Blanche**	The Lady Constance speakes not from her faith, But from her need.
	Constance	Oh, if thou grant my need, ⎫ Which onely lives but by the death of faith, That need, must needs inferre this principle,
145		That faith would live againe by death of need: O then tread downe my need, and faith mounts up, Keepe my need up, and faith is trodden downe.
	John	The king is movd, and answers not to this.
	Constance	O be remov'd from him, and answere well.
150	**Austria**	Doe so king Philip, hang no more in doubt.
	Bastard	Hang nothing but a Calves skin most sweet lout.
	France	I am perplext, and know not what to say.
	Pandulph	What canst thou say, but wil perplex thee more? If thou stand excommunicate, and curst?

[PCT] 1 Ff set an unusual speech-ending comma, emphasising the Bastard's interruption of Austria: most modern texts set the usual indication of interruption, a dash

[W] 2 F2 - 4 = 'That is', most modern texts = 'That's', F1 = 'That s'

155	**France**	Good reverend father, make my person yours,
		And tell me how you would bestow your selfe?[1]

[2] This royall hand and mine are newly knit,
And the conjunction of our inward soules
Married in league, coupled, and link'd together

160 With all religous strength of sacred vowes,
The latest breath that gave the sound of words
Was deepe-sworne faith, peace, amity, true love
Betweene our kingdomes and our royall selves,
And even before this truce, but new before,

165 No longer then we well could wash our hands,
To clap this royall bargaine up of peace,
Heaven [3] knowes they were besmear'd and over-staind
With slaughters pencill; where revenge did paint
The fearefull difference of incensed kings:

170 And shall these hands so lately purg'd of bloud?
So newly joyn'd in love? so strong in both,
Unyoke this seysure, and this kinde regreete?
Play fast and loose with faith? so jest with heaven,
Make such unconstant children of our [†4] selves

175 As now againe to snatch our palme from palme:
Un-sweare faith sworne, and on the marriage bed
Of smiling peace to march a bloody hoast,
And make a ryot on the gentle brow
Of true sincerity?

              O holy Sir

180 My reverend father, let it not be so;
Out of your grace, devise, ordaine, impose
Some gentle order, and then we shall be blest
To doe your pleasure, and continue friends.

185	**Pandulph**	All forme is formelesse, Order orderlesse,
		Save what is opposite to Englands love.

Therefore to Armes, be Champion of our Church,
Or let the Church our mother breathe her curse,
A mothers curse, on her revolting sonne:

190 France, thou maist hold a serpent by the tongue,

[PCT][1] the Ff setting of a question mark makes France's opening a (genuine?) call for help: surprisingly, some modern texts make it much more of an (arrogant) statement by setting a period instead

[SD][2] since by line 3. 1. 194 reference is made to France having taken John by the hand, some modern texts suggest he do so now

[▼3] Ff = 'Heaven', some modern texts = 'God'

[▼4] F2/most modern texts = 'our', F1 = 'onr'

		A cased [1] Lion by the mortall paw,	L 10 - c
		A fasting Tyger safer by the tooth,	
		Then keepe in peace that hand which thou dost hold.	

France   I may dis-joyne my hand, but not my faith.

95 **Pandulph**   So mak'st thou faith an enemy to faith,
And like a civill warre setst oath to oath,
Thy tongue against thy tongue.
O let thy vow
First made to heaven, first be to heaven perform'd,
200   That is, to be the Champion of our Church,
What since thou sworst, is sworne against thy selfe,
And may not be performed by thy selfe,
For that which thou hast sworne to doe amisse,
Is not amisse when it is truely done:
205   And being not done, where doing tends to ill,
The truth is then most done not doing it:
The better Act of purposes mistooke,
Is to mistake again, though indirect,
Yet indirection thereby growes direct,
210   And falshood, falshood cures, as fire cooles fire
Within the scorched veines of one new burn'd:

> [2] It is religion that doth make vowes kept,
> But thou hast sworne against religion:
> By what thou swear'st against the thing thou swear'st,
> 215   And mak'st an oath the suretie for thy truth, [3]
> Against an oath the truth, thou art unsure
> To sweare, sweares onely not to be forsworne,
> Else what a mockerie should it be to sweare?

But thou dost sweare, onely to be forsworne,
220   And most forsworne, to keepe what thou dost sweare,
Therefore thy later vowes, against thy first,
Is in thy selfe rebellion to thy selfe:

L 10 - c / R 10 - c : 3. 1. 259 - 289

[W] 1 Ff/some modern texts = 'cased', glosses include 'chafed', 'caged', 'chased' and 'crased'

[PCT] 2 in what is already a very dense passage Ff set non-grammatical punctuation which might suggest Pandulph is losing his self-assurance and rhetorical skills: most modern texts repunctuate for clarity; the most common example is
It is religion that doth make vowes kept;
But thou hast sworne against religion,
By what thou swear'st, against the thing thou swear'st,
And mak'st an oath the suretie for thy truth,
Against an oath. The truth thou art unsure
To sweare, sweares onely not to be forsworne -
Else what a mockerie should it be to sweare! -

[W] 3 Ff/most modern texts = 'truth', which one text emends to 'troth'

40

And better conquest never canst thou make,
Then arme thy constant and thy nobler parts
Against these giddy loose suggestions:
Upon which better part, our prayrs come in,
If thou vouchsafe them.
But if not, then know
The perill of our curses light on thee
So heavy, as thou shalt not shake them off
But in despaire, dye under their blacke weight.

Austria Rebellion, flat rebellion. }

Bastard Wil't not be?

Will not a Calves-skin stop that mouth of thine?

Dolphin Father, to Armes. }

Blanche Upon thy wedding day?

Against the blood that thou hast married?

What, shall our feast be kept with slaughtered men?

Shall braying trumpets, and loud churlish drums
Clamors of hell, be measures to our pomp?

O husband heare me: aye, alacke, how new
Is husband in my mouth? even for that name
Which till this time my tongue did nere pronounce;
Upon my knee I beg, goe not to Armes
[1] Against mine Uncle.

Constance O, upon my knee° made hard with kneeling,
I doe pray to thee,° thou vertuous Daulphin,
Alter not the doome° fore-thought by heaven. °

Blanche Now shall I see thy love, what motive may
Be stronger with thee, then the name of wife?

Constance That which upholdeth him, that thee upholds,
His Honor, Oh thine Honor, Lewis thine Honor.

Pandulph I muse your Majesty doth seeme so cold,
When such profound respects doe pull you on? [2]

R 10 - c : 3. 1. 290 - 318

LS [1] some modern texts follow Ff and set the text as shown, with a pause between the finish of Blanche's request and the start of Constance's: other modern texts restructure as the ° show, allowing Constance to jump in immediately and leaving the pause at the end of the speech for the Dolphin/Daulphin's and/or King of France's lack of response

PCT [2] Ff's setting of a question mark enables Pandulph to make his criticism seem less a condemnation but rather a 'genuine' moment of wonder: some modern texts replace the question mark with a much more pointed period

:55	Pandulph	I will denounce a curse upon his head.	
	France	Thou shalt not need.	
		England, I will fall frō¹ thee. ²	
	Constance	O faire returne of banish'd Majestie.	
	Eleanor	O foule revolt of French inconstancy.	
:60	John as England ³	France, ÿ⁴ shalt rue this houre within this houre.	R 10 - c
	Bastard	Old Time the clocke setter, ÿ⁵ bald sexton Time: Is it as he will? well then, France shall rue.	
	Blanche	The Sun's orecast with bloud: faire day adieu, Which is the side that I must goe withall?	
:65		I am with both, each Army hath a hand, And in their rage, I having hold of both, They whurle⁶ a-sunder, and dismember mee.	
:70		Husband, I cannot pray that thou maist winne: Uncle, I needs must pray that thou maist lose: Father, I may not wish the fortune thine: Grandam, I will not wish thy wishes thrive: Who-ever wins, on that side shall I lose: Assured losse, before the match be plaid.	
	Dolphin	Lady, with me, with me thy fortune lies. ⁷	
75	Blanche	There where my fortune lives, there my life dies.	
	˙John˙ ⁸	Cosen, goe draw our puisance together,⁹ France, I am burn'd up with inflaming wrath, A rage, whose heat hath this condition;	

ᴬᴮ ¹ F1 = 'frō', (printed as such because of lack of column width), F2/most modern texts = 'from'

ˢᴰ ² most modern texts suggest France now drops John's hand

ᴾ₃ quite fascinatingly, now that King Philip, as 'France' has formally disavowed any allegiance with King John, John's prefix now changes to 'England', a wonderful clue as to how he sees his next set of utterances and behaviour

ᴬᴮ ⁴ F1= 'ÿ', (printed as such because of lack of column width), F2/most modern texts = 'thou'

ᴬᴮ ⁵ F1 = 'ÿ', (printed as such because of lack of column width), F2/most modern texts = 'that'

ᵂ ⁶ Ff = 'whurle', which most modern texts set as 'whirl'

ᵂ ⁷ since Blanche uses the verb 'lives' in the next line, some modern texts suggest changing Ff's 'lies' to 'lives' so as to trigger her reply

ᵂᴴᴼ/ᴾ ⁸ most modern texts indicate this is said to the Bastard, and as John talks to someone who is essentially a family member, his prefix switches from 'England' to the personal 'John'

ˢᴰ ⁹ most modern texts indicate that the Bastard now exits

		That nothing can allay, nothing but blood,
280		The blood and deerest valued bloud of France.
	France	Thy rage shall burne thee up, & thou shalt turne
		To ashes, ere our blood shall quench that fire:
		Looke to thy selfe, thou art in jeopardie.
	John	No more then he that threats.
285		To Arms le'ts[1] hie.

[Exeunt]

---

[1] F1-2 = 'le'ts', F3/most modern texts = 'lets's'

Scœna Secunda [1]

ALLARUMS, EXCURSIONS: ENTER BASTARD WITH AUSTRIA'S HEAD [2]

Bastard Now by my life, this day grows wondrous hot,
 Some ayery Devill hovers in the skie,
 And pour's downe mischiefe.
       Austrias head lye there,

ENTER JOHN, ARTHUR, HUBERT

5 While Philip breathes.

John Hubert, keepe this boy: Philip make up,
 My Mother is assayled in our Tent,
 And tane I feare.

Bastard My Lord I rescued her,
10 Her Highnesse is in safety, feare you not:
 But on my Liege, for very little paines
 Will bring this labor to an happy end.

[Exit]
ALARUMS, EXCURSIONS, RETREAT. ENTER JOHN, ELEANOR, ARTHUR [3]
BASTARD, HUBERT, LORDS
[Most modern texts create a new scene here, Act Three Scene 3]

John [4] So shall it be: your Grace shall stay behinde
 So [5] strongly guarded: Cosen, looke not sad,
15 Thy Grandame loves thee, and thy Unkle will
 As deere be to thee, as thy father was.

Arthur O this will make my mother die with griefe.

COMP [1] this is the second time in this play F1 does not set a dividing line between the Act/Scene division and the text
SD [2] most modern texts suggest he is also carrying the lion's skin Austria wore
PCT [3] F2/most modern texts set a comma to separate the two characters: F1 sets no punctuation
WHO [4] most modern texts suggest the first two phrases are spoken to Eleanor, and the rest of the speech to Arthur
W [5] because of the previous scene, some commentators suggest altering Ff's 'So' to either 'More' or 'And'

John	[1] Cosen away for England, haste before,	
	And ere our comming see thou shake the bags	
20	Of hoording Abbots, [2] imprisoned angells	
	Set at libertie: the fat ribs of peace	
	Must by the hungry now be fed upon:	
	Use our Commission in his utmost force.	
Bastard	Bell, Booke, & Candle, shall not drive me back,	
25	When gold and silver becks me to come on.	
	I leave your highnesse: Grandame, I will pray	
	(If ever I remember to be holy)	
	For your faire safety: so I kisse your hand.	
Eleanor	Farewell gentle Cosen.	L 11 - c
	}	
30 **John**	Coz, farewell. [3]	
Eleanor	Come hether [4] little kinsman, harke, a worde.	
John	Come hether Hubert.	
	O my gentle Hubert,	
	We owe thee much: within this wall of flesh	
35	There is a soule counts thee her Creditor,	
	And with advantage meanes to pay thy love:	
	And my good friend, thy voluntary oath	
	Lives in this bosome, deerely cherished.	
	Give me thy hand, I had a thing to say,	
40	But I will fit it with some better tune. [5]	
	By heaven Hubert, I am almost asham'd	
	To say what good respect I have of thee.	
Hubert	I am much bounden to your Majesty.	
John	Good friend, thou hast no cause to say so yet,	
45	But thou shalt have: and creepe time nere so slow,	
	Yet it shall come, for me to doe thee good.	
	I had a thing to say, but let it goe:	

WHO [1] most modern texts suggest John says this to the Bastard

ALT [2] at least one commentator suggests moving the phrase 'imprisoned angells set at libertie' to before the last line of the speech

SD [3] most modern texts suggest the Bastard now leaves, and then Eleanor takes Arthur to one side allowing John a private word with Hubert: those modern texts who set Hubert as a character distinct from the Citizen of Angiers introduce him for the first time

W [4] Ff = 'hether', some modern texts set 'hither' both here and in the next line

W [5] Ff = 'tune', some modern texts = 'time'

The Sunne is in the heaven, and the proud day,
Attended with the pleasures of the world,
50   Is all too wanton, and too full of gawdes
To give me audience: If the mid-night bell
Did with his yron tongue, and brazen mouth
Sound on into the drowzie race [1] of night:
If this same were a Church-yard where we stand,
55   And thou possessed with a thousand wrongs:
Or if that surly spirit melancholy
Had bak'd thy bloud, and made it heavy, thicke,
Which else runnes tickling up and downe the veines,
Making that idiot laughter keepe mens eyes,
60   And straine their cheekes to idle merriment,
A passion hatefull to my purposes:
Or if that thou couldst see me without eyes,
Heare me without thine eares, and make reply
Without a tongue, using conceit alone,
65   Without eyes, eares, and harmefull sound of words:
Then, in despight of brooded watchfull day,
I would into thy bosome poure my thoughts:
But (ah) I will not, yet I love thee well,
And by my troth I thinke thou lov'st me well.

70   **Hubert**   So well, that what you bid me undertake,
Though that my death were adjunct to my Act,
By heaven I would doe it.

      John   Doe not I know thou would'st?

Good Hubert, Hubert, Hubert throw thine eye
75   On yon young boy: Ile tell thee what my friend,
He is a very serpent in my way,
And wheresoere this foot of mine doth tread,
He lies before me: dost thou understand me?

Thou art his keeper.

80   **Hubert**   And Ile keepe him so,
That he shall not offend your Majesty.

---

[1] Ff = 'race', most modern texts = 'ear'

John	Death.
Hubert	My Lord. [1] }
John	A Grave. }
85 Hubert	He shall not live. }
John	Enough. [2] }

I could be merry now,[3] Hubert, I love thee.

Well, Ile not say what I intend for thee:
Remember: Madam, Fare you well,
90 Ile send those powers o're to your Majesty.

Eleanor	My blessing goe with thee. ɴ }
John	For England Cosen, goe.

Hubert shall be your man, attend on you
With al true duetie: On toward Callice,[4] hoa.

[Exeunt]

R 11 - c

---

[1] ᴘᴄᴛ Ff are quite clear in setting this as a statement, suggesting Hubert understands straightaway: some modern texts soften the moment and character (anticipating his change of heart later?) by setting a question mark

[2] ʟs most modern texts tend to set these five short lines as one eleven syllable line: the Ff setting allows for silent , even tentative, moments between the two men as the revolting crime of child murder is broached

[3] ᴘᴄᴛ Ff set a comma, allowing John's delight/relief to break grammatical bounds: most modern texts reduce the moment by setting a period

[4] ɴ Ff = 'Callice', which most modern texts set as 'Calais'

47

Scœna Tertia
[Most modern texts terms this Act Three Scene 4]

ENTER FRANCE, DOLPHIN, PANDULPHO,[1] ATTENDANTS

France	So by a roaring Tempest on the flood,
	A whole Armado of convicted[2] saile
	Is scattered and dis-joyn'd from fellowship.
Pandulph	Courage and comfort, all shall yet goe well.
5 **France**	[3] What can goe well, when we have runne so ill?
	Are we not beaten? Is not Angiers lost?
	Arthur tane prisoner? divers deere friends slaine?
	And bloudy England into England gone,
	Ore-bearing interruption spight of France?
10 **Dolphin**	What he hath won, that hath he fortified :
	So hot a speed, with such advice dispos'd,
	Such temperate order in so fierce a cause,
	Doth want example : who hath read, or heard
	Of any kindred-action like to this?
15 **France**	Well could I beare that England had this praise,
	So we could finde some patterne of our shame :

ENTER CONSTANCE [4]

	Looke who comes heere? a grave unto a soule,
	Holding th'eternall spirit against her will,
	In the vilde prison of afflicted breath :
20	I prethee Lady goe away with me.
Constance	Lo ; now : now see the issue of your peace.
France	Patience good Lady, comfort gentle Constance.

[N][1] most modern texts set the name 'Pandulph', by which the character has been called throughout the play so far

[W][2] Ff/some modern texts = 'convicted', modern glosses include 'collected', 'conjuced', while one text sets 'consorted'

[PST][3] this speech could be set as anywhere between one and five sentences long

[SD][4] because of a later remark from France (line 62) some modern texts suggest Constance's hair is down: however, given her line 3. 3. 46 , there is the possibility she undoes her hair during the scene

Constance	No, I defie all Counsell, all redresse,
	But that which ends all counsell, true Redresse:
25	Death, death, O amiable, lovely death,
	Thou odoriferous stench: sound rottennesse,
	Arise forth from the couch of lasting night,
	Thou hate and terror to prosperitie,
	And I will kisse thy detestable bones,
30	And put my eye-balls in thy vaultie browes,
	And ring these fingers with thy houshold wormes,
	And stop this gap of breath with fulsome dust,
	And be a Carrion Monster like thy selfe;
	Come, grin on me, and I will thinke thou smil'st,
35	And buffe thee as thy wife: Miseries Love,
	O come to me.
France	O faire affliction, peace.⟩
Constance	No, no, I will not, having breath to cry:
	O that my tongue were in the thunders mouth,
40	Then with a passion would I shake the world,
	And rowze from sleepe that fell Anatomy
	Which cannot heare a Ladies feeble voyce,
	Which scornes a moderne [1] Invocation.
Pandulph	Lady, you utter madnesse, and not sorrow.
45 **Constance**	Thou art holy [2] to belye me so,
	I am not mad: this haire I teare is mine,
	My name is Constance, I was Geffreyes wife,
	Yong Arthur is my sonne, and he is lost:
	I am not mad, I would to heaven [3] I were,
50	For then 'tis like I should forget my selfe:
	O, if I could, what griefe should I forget?
	Preach some Philosophy to make me mad,
	And thou shalt be Canoniz'd (Cardinall.)
	For, being not mad, but sensible of greefe,
55	My reasonable part produces reason
	How I may be deliver'd of these woes,
	And teaches mee to kill or hang my selfe:
	If I were mad, I should forget my sonne,

L 12 - c

▼ [1] Ff/most modern texts = 'moderne': one fascinating gloss = 'mother's'

▼ [2] by setting 'holy', F1 - 3 offer a nine syllable line dripping in sarcasm: F4 sets the reprimand 'not holy', and creates pentameter: modern glosses = 'too holy' and 'unholy'

▼ [3] Ff = 'heaven', some modern texts = 'God'

		Or madly thinke a babe of clowts were he:
60		I am not mad : too well, too well I feele
		The different plague of each calamitie.
	France	Binde up those tresses : O what love I note
		In the faire multitude of those her haires ;
		Where but by chance a silver drop hath falne.
65		Even to that drop ten thousand wiery fiends [1]
		Doe glew themselves in sociable griefe,
		Like true, inseparable, faithfull loves,
		Sticking together in calamitie.
	Constance	To England, if you will.
70	**France**	Binde up your haires.
	Constance	Yes that I will : and wherefore will I do it?
		I tore them from their bonds, and cride aloud,
		[2] O, that these hands could so redeeme my sonne,
		As they have given these hayres their libertie :
75		But now I envie at their libertie,
		And will againe commit them to their bonds,
		Because my poore childe is a prisoner.
		And Father Cardinall, I have heard you say
		That we shall see and know our friends in heaven :
80		If that be true, I shall see my boy againe ;
		For since the birth of Caine, the first male-childe
		To him that did but yesterday suspire,
		There was not such a gracious creature borne :
		But now will Canker-sorrow eat my bud,
85		And chase the native beauty from his cheeke,
		And he will looke as hollow as a Ghost,
		As dim and meager as an Agues fitte,
		And so hee'll dye : and rising so againe,
		When I shall meet him in the Court of heaven
90		I shall not know him : therefore never, never
		Must I behold my pretty Arthur more.
	Pandulph	You hold too heynous a respect of greefe.
	Constance	He talkes to me, that never had a sonne.
	France	You are as fond of greefe, as of your childe.

---

[1] Ff = 'fiends', most modern texts = 'friends'

[2] most modern texts set this and the following line in quotation marks

Constance
Greefe fils the roome up of my absent childe:
Lies in his bed, walkes up and downe with me,
Puts on his pretty lookes, repeats his words,
Remembers[†1] me of all his gracious parts,
Stuffes out his vacant garments with his forme:
Then, have I reason to be fond of griefe?

Fareyouwell: [†2] had you such a losse as I,
I could give better comfort then you doe.

I will not keepe this forme upon my head,[3]
When there is such disorder in my witte:
O Lord, my boy, my Arthur, my faire sonne,
My life, my joy, my food, my all the world:
My widow-comfort, and my sorrowes cure.

[Exit]

France
I feare some out-rage, and Ile follow her.

[Exit]

Dolphin
There's nothing in this world can make me joy,
Life is as tedious as a twice-told tale,
Vexing the dull eare of a drowsie man;
And bitter shame hath spoyl'd the sweet words [4] taste,
That it yeelds nought but shame and bitternesse.

Pandulph
Before the curing of a strong disease,
Even in the instant of repaire and health,
The fit is strongest: Evils that take leave
On their departure,[5] most of all shew evill:
What have you lost by losing of this day?

Dolphin
All daies of glory, joy, and happinesse.

Pandulph
If you had won it, certainely you had.

No, no: when Fortune meanes to men most good,
Shee lookes upon them with a threatning eye:
'Tis strange to thinke how much King John hath lost
In this which he accounts so clearely wonne: R 12 - c
Are you not griev'd that Arthur is his prisoner?

R 12 - c / L 13 - c : 3. 4. 93 - 123

[W 1] F2/most modern texts = 'Remembers', F1 = 'Remembets'

[W 2] F2/most modern texts = 'Fare you well', F1 = 'Fareyouwell'

[SD 3] some modern texts suggest she again tears at her hair

[W 4] Ff = 'words', some modern texts = 'world's'

[PCT 5] some modern texts follow F4 and transfer the comma from here to the end of the previous line

Dolphin	As heartily as he is glad he hath him.
Pandulph	Your minde is all as youthfull as your blood.

Now heare me speake with a propheticke spirit:
For even the breath of what I meane to speake,
30   Shall blow each dust, each straw, each little rub
Out of the path which shall directly lead
Thy foote to Englands Throne.
                 And therefore marke:
John hath seiz'd Arthur, and it cannot be,
35   That whiles warme life playes in that infants veines,
The mis-plac'd-John should entertaine an [1] houre,
One minute, nay one quiet breath of rest.

A Scepter snatch'd with an unruly hand,
Must be as boysterously maintain'd as gain'd.

40 And he that stands upon a slipp'ry place,
Makes nice of no vilde hold to stay him up:
That John may stand, then Arthur needs must fall,
So be it, for it cannot be but so.

Dolphin	But what shall I gaine by yong Arthurs fall?
45 **Pandulph**	You, in the right of Lady Blanch your wife,

May then make all the claime that Arthur did.

Dolphin	And loose it, life and all, as Arthur did.
Pandulph	How green you are, and fresh in this old world?

John layes you plots: the times conspire with you,
50   For he that steepes his safetie in true blood,
Shall finde but bloodie safety, and untrue.

This Act so evilly [2] borne shall coole the hearts
Of all his people, and freeze up their zeale,
That none so small advantage shall step forth
55   To checke his reigne, but they will cherish it.

No naturall exhalation in the skie,
No scope of Nature, no distemper'd day,
No common winde, no customed event,
But they will plucke away his naturall cause,
60   And call them Meteors, prodigies, and signes,
Abbortives, presages, and tongues of heaven,
Plainly denouncing vengeance upon John.

---

[1] Ff = 'an', one commentator makes the sensible suggestion of setting 'one' to match the rhetorical repetition in the following line

[2] Ff/most modern texts = 'so evilly', one modern text sets 'so vilely'

Dolphin		May be he will not touch yong Arthurs life,
		But hold himselfe safe in his prisonment.
165	**Pandulph**	O Sir, when he shall heare of your approach,
		If that yong Arthur be not gone alreadie,
		Even at that newes he dies : and then the hearts
		Of all his people shall revolt from him,
		And kisse the lippes of unacquainted change,
170		And picke strong matter of revolt, and wrath
		Out of the bloody fingers ends of John.

Me thinkes I see this hurley all on foot;
And O, what better matter breeds for you,
Then I have nam'd.
                    The Bastard Falconbridge
175   Is now in England ransacking the Church,
Offending Charity : If but a dozen French
Were there in Armes, they would be as a Call
To traine ten thousand English to their side;
180   Or, as a little snow, tumbled about,
Anon becomes a Mountaine.
                      O noble Dolphine,
Go with me to the King, 'tis wonderfull,
What may be wrought out of their discontent,
185   Now that their soules are topfull of offence,[1]
For England go; I will whet on the King.

Dolphin		Strong reasons makes strange [2] actions : let us go,
		If you say I, the King will not say no.

[Exeunt]

L 13 - b

PCT [1] Ff set a comma, allowing Pandulph to run on startlingly swiftly from one idea to the next: most modern texts set a period

W [2] with the various options available most modern texts still set F1's 'makes strange': Ff = 'makes', one modern gloss = 'make': F1 = 'strange', F2 = 'strong'

Actus Quartus,[1] Scæna prima

ENTER HUBERT AND EXECUTIONERS [2]

Hubert	Heate me these Irons hot, and looke thou stand
	Within the Arras: when I strike my foot
	Upon the bosome of the ground, rush forth
	And binde the boy, which you shall finde with me
5	Fast to the chaire: be heedfull: hence, and watch.
Executioner{s}[3]	I hope your warrant will beare out the deed.
Hubert	Uncleanly scruples feare not you: looke too't.
	Yong Lad come forth; I have to say with you.

ENTER ARTHUR

Arthur	Good morrow Hubert.
10 Hubert	Good morrow, little Prince.⁾
Arthur	As little Prince, having so great a Title
	To be more Prince, as may be: you are sad.
Hubert	Indeed I have beene merrier.
Arthur	'Mercie on me:⁾
15	Me thinkes no body should be sad but I:
	Yet I remember, when I was in France,
	Yong Gentlemen would be as sad as night
	Onely for wantonnesse: by my Christendome,
	So I were out of prison, and kept Sheepe
20	I should be as [4] merry as the day is long:
	And so I would be heere, but that I doubt
	My Unckle practises more harme to me:

---

^{COMP} 1 F1 sets 'Actus Quartus' twice, here and page 75: most modern texts accept this as the 'genuine' Act Four

^{SD} 2 because of the ensuing dialogue, some modern texts suggest they bring in irons and a rope

^P 3 Ff set a prefix which could refer to one or more characters, viz. 'Exec.', which could be singular or plural: most modern texts assign all speeches so marked to a single executioner, though more different characters could speak at different times: also, most modern texts suggest the Executioner{s} withdraw{s} at the end of the line

^W 4 Ff set an eleven syllable line, (perhaps suggesting Arthur slightly onrushing at the joy of the idea): some modern texts suggest omitting Ff's 'as'

He is affraid of me, and I of him:
Is it my fault, that I was Geffreyes sonne?

25   No in deede [1] is't not: and I would to heaven [2]
I were your sonne, so you would love me, Hubert: [3]

Hubert   [4] If I talke to him, with his innocent prate
He will awake my mercie, which lies dead:
Therefore I will be sodaine, and dispatch.

30   **Arthur**   Are you sicke Hubert?   you looke pale to day,
Insooth I would you were a little sicke,
That I might sit all night, and watch with you.

I warrant I love you more then you do me.

Hubert   His words do take possession of my bosome.

35   [5] Reade heere yong Arthur. †[6]
How now foolish rheume?

Turning dispitious torture out of doore?

I must be breefe, least [7] resolution drop
Out at mine eyes, in tender womanish teares.

40   Can you not reade it?
Is it not faire writ?

Arthur   Too fairely Hubert, for so foule effect, [8]
Must you with hot Irons, burne out both mine eyes?

Hubert   Yong Boy, I must.
}

45   **Arthur**   And will you?
}

Hubert   And I will. [9]

---

[w]1 by setting the two words 'in deede' separately, Ff show Arthur being capable of a rather naughty pun, a fine tribute to his spirit given the circumstances of his imprisonment: most modern texts set 'indeed'

[w]2 Ff = 'heaven', some modern texts = 'God'

[PCT]3 F1 - 3 set a colon, as if Hubert's private concerns force him to cut off Arthur's prattle: F4/most modern texts set a period

[A]4 most modern texts suggest that this speech for Hubert and all of his next (save the second, and the last two sentences) are asides

[SD]5 most modern texts suggest Hubert shows Arthur the warrant

[w]6 F1 = 'Arthnr', F2/most modern texts = 'Arthur'

[w]7 F4/most modern texts = 'lest', F1 - 3 = 'least'

[PCT]8 Ff set a comma, suggesting the horror of the image pushes Arthur quickly from one thought to the next: most modern texts suggest more self-control for the boy by setting a period or major punctuation

[LS]9 most modern texts set these three short lines as one ten syllable line, thus removing Ff's potential hesitations inherent in Hubert's responses to Arthur's direct questions

55

Arthur	Have you the heart?
	When your head did but
	ake,
50	I knit my hand-kercher about your browes
	(The best I had, a Princesse wrought it me)
	And I did never aske it you againe :
	And with my hand, at midnight held your head ;
	And like the watchfull minutes, to the houre,
55	Still and anon cheer'd up the heavy time ;
	Saying, what lacke you? and where lies your greefe?
	Or what good love may I performe for you?
	Many a poore mans sonne would have lyen still,
	And nere have spoke a loving word to you :
60	But you, at your sicke service had a Prince :
	Nay, you may thinke my love was craftie love,
	And call it cunning.
	If heaven be pleas'd that you must use me ill,
	Why then you must.
65	Will you put out mine eyes?
	These eyes, that never did, nor never shall
	So much as frowne on you. [1]
Hubert	I have sworne to do it :
	And with hot Irons must I burne them out.
70 **Arthur**	Ah, none but in this Iron Age, would do it :
	The Iron of it selfe, though heate red hot,
	Approaching neere these eyes, would drinke my teares,
	And quench this [2] fierie indignation,
	Even in the matter [3] of mine innocence :
75	Nay, after that, consume away in rust,
	But for containing fire to harme mine eye :
	Are you more stubborne hard, then hammer'd Iron?
	And if an Angell should have come to me,
	And told me Hubert should put out mine eyes,
80	I would not have beleev'd him : no tongue but Huberts.
Hubert	[4] Come forth : Do as I bid you do.

R 13 - b

R 13 - b / L 14 - b : 4. 1. 41 - 71

[PCT] [1] Ff suggest a reflection or statement by setting a period: many modern texts weaken the moment by setting a question mark

[W] [2] Ff = 'this': most modern texts set 'his', while glosses include 'its' and 'their'

[W] [3] Ff/most modern texts = 'matter', one interesting gloss = 'water'

[SD] [4] most modern texts suggest Hubert stamps on the floor, the agreed upon signal for the entry of the Executioners, who then come forward with the various items of their trade (at the very least the ropes and irons seen earlier)

56

Arthur	O save me Hubert, save me : my eyes are out Even with the fierce lookes of these bloody men.
Hubert	Give me the Iron I say, and binde him heere.
Arthur	Alas, what neede you be so boistrous rough?
85	I will not struggle, I will stand stone still : For heaven [1] sake Hubert let me not be bound : Nay heare me Hubert, drive these men away, And I will sit as quiet as a Lambe.
90	I will not stirre, not winch,[2] nor speake a word, Nor looke upon the Iron angerly : Thrust but these men away, and Ile forgive you, What ever torment you do put me too.
Hubert	Go stand within : let me alone with him.
Executioner{s} [3]	I am best pleas'd to be from such a deede.
95 **Arthur**	Alas, I then have chid away my friend, He hath a sterne looke, but a gentle heart : Let him come backe, that his compassion may Give life to yours.
Hubert	Come (Boy) prepare your selfe. ⟩
100 **Arthur**	Is there no remedie?
Hubert	None, but to lose your eyes. ⟩
Arthur	O heaven : [4] that there were but a moth [5] in yours, A graine, a dust, a gnat, a wandering haire, Any annoyance in that precious sense : Then feeling what small things are boysterous there, Your vilde intent must needs seeme horrible.
105	
Hubert	Is this your promise? Go too, hold your toong [6]

---

[1] Ff = 'heaven', some modern texts = 'God's'

[2] F2/most modern texts = 'wince', F1 = 'winch'

[3] see footnote #3, page 54: also, most modern texts suggest the Executioner{s} leave at the end of the line

[4] Ff = 'heaven', some modern texts = 'God'

[5] Ff = 'moth' which most modern texts set as 'mote'

[6] F1 sets no punctuation, as if Hubert interrupts him: F2/most modern texts set a period

Arthur	Hubert, the utterance of a brace of tongues,
110	Must needes want pleading for a paire of eyes:
	Let me not hold my tongue: let me not Hubert,
	Or Hubert, if you will cut out my tongue,
	So I may keepe mine eyes.
	O spare mine eyes,
115	Though to no use, but still to looke on you.
	Loe, by my troth, the Instrument is cold,
	And would not harme me.
	}
Hubert	I can heate it, Boy.
Arthur	No, in good sooth: the fire is dead with griefe,
120	Being create for comfort, to be us'd
	In undeserved extreames: See else your selfe,
	There is no malice in this burning cole,
	The breath of heaven, hath blowne his spirit out,
	And strew'd repentant ashes on his head.
125 Hubert	But with my breath I can revive it Boy.
Arthur	And if you do, you will but make it blush,
	And glow with shame of your proceedings, Hubert:
	Nay, it perchance will sparkle in your eyes:
	And, like a dogge that is compell'd to fight,
130	Snatch at his Master that doth tarre him on.
	All things that you should use to do me wrong
	Deny their office: onely you do lacke
	That mercie, which fierce fire, and Iron extends,
	Creatures of note for mercy, lacking uses.
135 Hubert	Well, see to live: I will not touch thine eye,
	For all the Treasure that thine Unckle owes,
	Yet am I sworne, and I did purpose, Boy,
	With this same very Iron, to burne them out.
Arthur	O now you looke like Hubert.
140	All this while
	You were disguis'd.
	}
Hubert	Peace: no more.
	Adieu,
	Your Unckle must not know but you are dead.
145	Ile fill these dogged Spies with false reports:
	And, pretty childe, sleepe doubtlesse, and secure,

L 14 - b

                 That Hubert for the wealth of all the world,
                 Will not offend thee.
                                }

Arthur   O heaven! [1]

150   I thanke you Hubert.

Hubert   Silence, no more;   go closely in with mee,
                 Much danger do I undergo for thee.

                        [Exeunt]

---

[w] [1] Ff = 'heaven', some modern texts = 'God!'

Scena Secunda

ENTER JOHN,[1] **PEMBROKE, SALISBURY, AND OTHER LORDES**

John   Heere once againe we sit: once against crown'd [2]
         And look'd upon, I hope, with chearefull eyes.

Pembroke   This once again (but that your Hignes pleas'd)
         Was once superfluous: you were Crown'd before,
5   And that high Royalty was nere pluck'd off:
         The faiths of men, nere stained with revolt:
         Fresh expectation troubled not the Land
         With any long'd-for-change, or better State.

Salisbury   Therefore, to be possess'd with double pompe,
10   To guard [3] a Title, that was rich before;
         To gilde refined Gold, to paint the Lilly;
         To throw a perfume on the Violet,
         To smooth the yce, or adde another hew
         Unto the Raine-bow; or with Taper-light
15   To seeke the beauteous eye of heaven to garnish,
         Is wastefull, and ridiculous excesse.

Pembroke   But that your Royall pleasure must be done,
         This[†4] acte, is as an ancient tale new told,
         And, in the last repeating, troublesome,
20   Being urged at a time unseasonable.

Salisbury   In this the Anticke,[5] and well noted face
         Of plaine old forme, is much disfigured,
         And like a shifted winde unto a saile,
         It makes the course of thoughts to fetch about,
25   Startles, and frights consideration:
         Makes sound opinion sicke, and truth suspected,
         For putting on so new a fashion'd robe.

SD [1] because of the first speech, some modern texts suggest John has just been crowned and is seated on his throne in full coronation regalia

W [2] F3/most modern texts = 'once again crown'd': F1 - 2 = 'once against crown'd'

W [3] Ff/most modern texts = 'guard', one excellent recent gloss = 'gaud'

W [4] F2/most modern texts = 'This', F1 = 'Thi s'

W [5] Ff = 'Anticke', which most modern texts set as 'antique'

Pembroke	When Workemen strive to do better then wel,	
	They do confound their skill in covetousnesse,	
30	And oftentimes excusing of a fault,	
	Doth make the fault the worse by th'excuse: ¹	
	As patches set upon a little breach,	
	Discredite more in hiding of the fault,	
	Then did the fault before it was so patch'd.	

35	**Salisbury**	To this effect, before you were new crown'd
		We breath'd our Councell: but it pleas'd your Highnes
		To over-beare it, and we are all well pleas'd,
		Since all, and every part of what we would
		Doth make a stand, at what your Highnesse will.

R 14 - b

40	**John**	Some reasons of this double Corronation
		I have possest you with, and thinke them strong.

And more, more strong, then lesser ² is my feare
I shall indue you with: Meane time, but aske
What you would have reform'd. ³ that is not well,
45 And well shall you perceive, how willingly
I will both heare, and grant you your requests.

Pembroke	Then I, as one that am the tongue of these
	To sound the purposes of all their hearts,
	Both for my selfe, and them: but chiefe of all
50	Your safety: for the which, my selfe and them
	Bend their best studies, heartily request
	Th'infranchisement of Arthur, whose restraint
	Doth move the murmuring lips of discontent
	To breake into this dangerous argument.

55 If what in rest you have, in right you hold,
Why then your feares, which (as they say) attend

The steppes of wrong, should move you to mew up
Your tender kinsman, and to choake his dayes
With barbarous ignorance, and deny his youth
60 The rich advantage of good exercise,
That the times enemies may not have this
To grace occasions: let it be our suite,
That you have bid us aske his libertie,

R 14 - b / L 15 - b : 4. 2. 28 - 66

ᵂ ₁ since Ff set a nine syllable line, most modern texts set either 'the worse by the excuse' or 'the worser by th'excuse'

ᵂ ₂ Ff = 'then lesser': many glosses abound, the most often adopted being 'than lesser' or 'when lesser': also offered are 'the lesser', 'the less that' and F2's 'then less'

ᴾᶜᵀ ₃ F1 sets a peculiar period which F2/most modern texts replace with a comma

Which for our goods, we do no further aske,
65   Then, whereupon our weale on you depending,
Counts it your weale :   he have his liberty. [1]

ENTER HUBERT

John   Let it be so :   I do commit his youth
To your direction :   Hubert, what newes with you? [2]

Pembroke   This is the man should do the bloody deed :
70   He shew'd his warrant to a friend of mine,
The image of a wicked heynous fault
Lives in his eye :   that close aspect of his,
Do [3] shew the mood of a much troubled brest,
And I do fearefully beleeve 'tis done,
75   What we so fear'd he had a charge to do.

Salisbury   The colour of the King doth come, and go
Betweene his purpose and his conscience,
Like Heralds 'twixt two dreadfull battailes set :
His passion is so ripe, it needs must breake.

80 **Pembroke**   And when it breakes, I feare will issue thence
The foule corruption of a sweet childes death.

John   [4] We cannot hold mortalities strong hand.

Good Lords, although my will to give, is living,
The suite which you demand is gone, and dead.

85   He tels us Arthur is deceas'd to night.

Salisbury   Indeed we fear'd his sicknesse was past cure.

L 15 - b :   4. 2. 67 - 86

[PCT 1] Ff's less than grammatical punctuation could suggest Pembroke is getting somewhat flustered in the final part of his request: most modern texts punctuate somewhat more logically, along the lines of

The steppes of wrong, should move you to mew up
Your tender kinsman, and to choake his dayes
With barbarous ignorance, and deny his youth
The rich advantage of good exercise?
That the times enemies may not have this
To grace occasions, let it be our suite,
That you have bid us aske, his libertie,
Which for our goods, we do no further aske
Than whereupon our weale on you depending,
Counts it your weale he have his liberty.

while much clearer, the repunctuation reduces both the awkwardness and the final four word firm demand of the original

[SD 2] most modern texts suggest Hubert and John move aside

[W 3] F1 - 3 = 'Do', F4 = 'Does', some modern texts = 'Doth'

[SD 4] most modern texts suggest John now comes back to the Lords and speaks to them

Pembroke	Indeed we heard how neere his death he was,
	Before the childe himselfe felt he was sicke :
	This must be answer'd either heere, or hence.
John	Why do you bend such solemne browes on me?
	Thinke you I beare the Sheeres of destiny?
	Have I commandement on the pulse of life?
Salisbury	It is apparant foule-play, and 'tis shame
	That Greatnesse should so grossely offer it ;
	So thrive it in your game,[1] and so farewell.
Pembroke	Stay yet (Lord Salisbury) Ile go with thee,
	And finde th'inheritance of this poore childe,
	His little kingdome of a forced grave.
	That blood which ow'd the bredth of all this Ile,
	Three foot of it doth hold ; bad world the while :
	This must not be thus borne, this will breake out
	To all our sorrowes, and ere long I doubt.

[Exeunt]

John	They burn in indignation : I repent :

[Enter Mes{senger}] [2]

	There is no sure foundation set on blood :	L 15 - b
	No certaine life atchiev'd by others death :	
	A fearefull eye thou hast.	
	Where is that blood,	
	That I have seene inhabite in those cheekes?	
	So foule a skie, cleeres not without a storme,	
	Poure downe thy weather : how goes all in France?	
Messenger	From France to England,[3] never such a powre	
	For any forraigne preparation,	
	Was levied in the body of a land.	

PCT [1] most modern texts replace Ff's comma with the ubiquitous and overworked exclamation point: Ff's setting allows Salisbury a firm disavowal of all John stands for, without unnecessary histrionics

UE [2] this is an unusual entry in that being set at the right of the column, alongside the text (probably a Playhouse set direction) it could suggest that either the Messenger does not wish to draw attention to himself, and/or that the on-stage action is as important as the entry itself, which given what John is saying would certainly be the situation here: this would also explain why John does not take notice of the Messenger until two lines after the entry: most modern texts delay the entry by two lines

PCT [3] Ff's comma extraordinarily concisely establishes the Messenger's sense of urgency : most modern texts replace it with a grammatically correct period

|15 | | The Copie of your speede is learn'd by them :
For when you should be told they do prepare,
The tydings comes, that they are all arriv'd. |

John   ¹ Oh where hath our Intelligence bin drunke?

Where hath it slept?

              Where is my Mothers care? ²

|20   That such an Army could be drawne in France,

And she not heare of it?
            }

Messenger   My Liege, her eare

Is stopt with dust :   the first of April di'de

Your noble mother ;   and as I heare, my Lord,

|25   The Lady Constance in a frenzie di'de

Three dayes before :   but this from Rumors tongue

I idely heard :   if true, or false I know not.

John   With-hold thy speed, dreadfull Occasion :

O make a league with me, 'till I have pleas'd

|30   My discontented Peeres.

                 What?

                      Mother dead?

How wildely then walkes my Estate in France?

Under whose conduct came those powres of France,

|35   That thou for truth giv'st out are landed heere?

Messenger   Under the Dolphin.

ENTER BASTARD AND PETER OF POMFRET

John   Thou hast made me giddy

With these ill tydings :   Now?   What sayes the world

To your proceedings?

                      Do not seeke to stuffe

|40   My head with more ill newes :   for it is full.

Bastard   But if you be a-feard to heare the worst,

Then let the worst un-heard, fall on your head.

John   Beare with me Cosen, for I was amaz'd

|45   Under the tide ;   but now I breath againe

Aloft the flood, and can give audience

To any tongue, speake it of what it will.

ᴵˢᵀ ₁ this speech could be set any where between one and four sentences

ᵂ ₂ in view of the upcoming image, some commentators suggest altering Ff's 'care?' to 'ear?'

Bastard		How I have sped among the Clergy men,
		The summes I have collected shall expresse :
150		But as I travail'd [1] hither through the land,
		I finde the people strangely fantasied,
		Possest with rumors, full of idle dreames,
		Not knowing what they feare, but full of feare.

And here's a Prophet that I brought with me
From forth the streets of Pomfret, whom I found
With many hundreds treading on his heeles :
To whom he sung in rude harsh sounding rimes,
That ere the next Ascension day at noone,
Your Highnes should deliver up your Crowne.

John Thou idle Dreamer, wherefore didst thou so?

Peter Fore-knowing that the truth will fall out so.

John Hubert, away with him : imprison him,
And on that day at noone, whereon he sayes
I shall yeeld up my Crowne, let him be hang'd.

Deliver him to safety, and returne,
For I must use thee. [2]
　　　　　　O my gentle Cosen,
Hear'st thou the newes abroad, who are arriv'd?

Bastard The French (my Lord) mens mouths are ful of it :
Besides I met Lord Bigot, and Lord Salisburie
With eyes as red as new enkindled fire,
And others more, going to seeke the grave

Of Arthur, whom they say is kill'd to night,° on your suggestion. [†]

John Gentle kinsman, go °[3]

And thrust thy selfe into their Companies,　　　　R 15 - b
I have a way to winne their loves againe :
Bring them before me.
　　　　　　　　　}
Bastard I will seeke them out.

John Nay, but make haste : the better foote before.
O, let me have no subject enemies,

[1] F1 - 3 = 'travail'd', F4/some modern texts = 'travel'd', thus reducing the enormity of the Bastard's imagery

[2] most modern texts indicate Hubert takes away the Prophet

[3] seen at the bottom of page #15 of the History section, most modern texts suggest there was insufficient room to set this passage as three lines, hence the two irregular Ff lines (15/5 syllables): while this may be so, the complete speech for the Bastard is irregular, and the explosion on the line virtually demanding John clear himself of any complicity in Arthur's supposed death is perfectly understandable given the Bastard's often demonstrated impetuous nature

		When adverse Forreyners affright my Townes With dreadfull pompe of stout invasion.
		Be Mercurie, set feathers to thy heeles, And flye (like thought) from them, to me againe.
85	**Bastard**	The spirit of the time shall teach me speed.

[Exit]

	John	Spoke like a sprightfull Noble Gentleman.
		Go after him: for he perhaps shall neede Some Messenger betwixt me, and the Peeres,

And be thou hee.

90	**Messenger**	With all my heart, my Liege. [1]
	John	My mother dead? [2]

ENTER HUBERT

Hubert	My Lord, they say five Moones were seene to night: [†] Foure fixed, and the fift did whirle about

The other foure, in wondrous motion.

95	John	Five Moones?
	Hubert	Old men, and Beldames, in the streets [3]

	Do prophesie upon it dangerously: Yong Arthurs death is common in their mouths, And when they talke of him, they shake their heads,
:00	And whisper one another in the eare.
	And he that speakes, doth gripe the hearers wrist, Whilst he that heares, makes fearefull action With wrinkled browes, with nods, with rolling eyes.
	I saw a Smith stand with his hammer (thus)
:05	The whilst his Iron did on the Anvile coole, With open mouth swallowing a Taylors newes, Who with his Sheeres, and Measure in his hand, Standing on slippers, which his nimble haste Had falsely thrust upon contrary feete,
:10	Told of a many thousand warlike French, That were embattailed, and rank'd in Kent.
	Another leane, unwash'd Artificer, Cuts off his tale, and talkes of Arthurs death.

[SD] [1] most modern texts indicate the Messenger now exits

[LS] [2] the actor has choice as to which two of these three short lines may be joined as one line of split verse

[LS] [3] the actor has choice as to which two of these three short lines may be joined as one line of split verse

John	Why seek'st thou to possesse me with these feares?
15	Why urgest thou so oft yong Arthurs death?
	Thy hand hath murdred him : I had a mighty cause
	To wish him dead, but thou hadst none to kill him.

| Hubert | No had [1] (my Lord?) why, did you not provoke me? |

John	It is the curse of Kings, to be attended
20	By slaves, that take their humors for a warrant,
	To breake within the bloody house of life,
	And on the winking of Authoritie
	To understand a Law ; to know the meaning
	Of dangerous Majesty, when perchance it frownes
25	More upon humor, then advis'd respect.

| Hubert | Heere is your hand and Seale for what I did. [2] |

John	Oh, when the last accompt twixt heaven & earth
	Is to be made, then shall this hand and Seale
	Witnesse against us to damnation.
30	How oft the sight of meanes to do ill deeds,
	Make deeds ill done?
	Had'st not thou beene by,
	A fellow by the hand of Nature mark'd,
	Quoted, and sign'd to do a deede of shame,
35	This murther had not come into my minde.
	But taking note of thy abhorr'd Aspect,
	Finding thee fit for bloody villanie :
	Apt, liable to be employ'd in danger,
	I faintly broke with thee of Arthurs death :
40	And thou, to be endeered to a King,
	Made it no conscience to destroy a Prince.

L 16 - b

| Hubert | My Lord. [3] |

John	Had'st thou but shooke thy head, or made a pause
	When I spake darkely, what I purposed :
45	Or turn'd an eye of doubt upon my face ;
	As bid me tell my tale in expresse words :
	Deepe shame had struck me dumbe, made me break off,
	And those thy feares, might have wrought feares in me.

[W] [1] Ff/most modern texts = 'No had': to clarify the archaic construction, one gloss = 'Had none?'

[SD] [2] most modern texts suggest Hubert now shows the warrant he received from John

[PCT] [3] most modern texts replace Ff's period with a dash, suggesting John interrupt Hubert

But, thou didst understand me by my signes,
50 And didst in signes againe parley with sinne,
Yea, without stop, didst let thy heart consent,
And consequently, thy rude hand to acte
The deed, which both our tongues held vilde to name.

Out of my sight, and never see me more:
55 My Nobles leave me, and my State is braved,
Even at my gates, with rankes of forraigne powres;
Nay, in the body of this fleshly Land,
This kingdome, this Confine of blood, and breathe [1]
Hostilitie, and civill tumult reignes
60 Betweene my conscience, and my Cosins death.

Hubert   Arme you against your other enemies:
Ile make a peace betweene your soule, and you.

Yong Arthur is alive: This hand of mine
Is yet[2] a maiden, and an innocent hand. [3]

65 Not painted with the Crimson spots of blood,
Within this bosome, never entred yet
The dreadfull motion of a murderous thought,
And you have slander'd Nature in my forme,
Which howsoever rude exteriorly,
70 Is yet the cover of a fayrer minde,
Then to be butcher of an innocent childe.

John   Doth Arthur live?
            O hast thee to the Peeres,
Throw this report on their incensed rage,
And make them tame to their obedience.

Forgive the Comment that my passion made
Upon thy feature, for my rage was blinde,
And foule immaginarie eyes of blood
Presented thee more hideous then thou art.

80 Oh, answer not; but to my Closset bring
The angry Lords, with all expedient hast,
I conjure thee but slowly: run more fast.

[Exeunt]

W/PCT [1] F1 - 2 = 'breathe', F3 = 'breath', to which most modern texts add F4's comma

W [2] F1 = 'Isyet', F2/most modern texts = 'Is yet'

PCT [3] F1 sets a period, perhaps suggesting the horrific thought gives Hubert a needed (ungrammatical) break:
F2/most modern texts set a comma

Scœna Tertia

ENTER ARTHUR ON THE WALLES [1]

Arthur	The Wall is high, and yet will I leape downe.
	Good ground be pittifull, and hurt me not:
	There's few or none do know me, if they did,
	This Ship-boyes semblance hath disguis'd me quite.
5	I am afraide, and yet Ile venture it.
	If I get downe, and do not breake my limbes,
	Ile finde a thousand shifts to get away;
	As good to dye, and go; as dye, and stay. [2]
	Oh me, my Unckles spirit is in these stones,
10	Heaven take my soule, and England keep my bones.

[Dies]

ENTER PEMBROKE, SALISBURY, & BIGOT

Salisbury	Lords, I will meet him at S. Edmondsbury,
	It is our safetie, and we must embrace
	This gentle offer of the perillous time.
Pembroke	Who brought that Letter from the Cardinall?
15 Salisbury	The Count Meloone,[3] a Noble Lord of France,
	Whose private with me [4] of the Dolphines love,
	Is much more generall, then these lines import. R 16 - b
Bigot	To morrow morning let us meete him then.
Salisbury	Or rather then set forward, for 'twill be
20	Two long dayes journey (Lords) or ere we meete.

ENTER BASTARD

R 16 - b / L 17 - b : 4. 3. 1 - 20

[SD 1] because of the fourth line of the opening speech, most modern texts indicate he is disguised as a cabin-boy

[SD 2] most modern texts indicate he now leaps

[N/P 3] Ff set variations of 'Meloone', 'Meloon', or 'Melloone' throughout, which most modern texts set as 'Melun': this is the only time this text will note the variation

[W 4] Ff/most modern texts = 'private with me': the modern gloss making most sense = 'private warrant'

	Bastard	Once more to day well met, distemper'd Lords,
		The King by me requests your presence straight.
	Salisbury	The king hath dispossest himselfe of us,
		We will not lyne his thin-bestained [1] cloake
25		With our pure Honors: nor attend the foote
		That leaves the print of blood where ere it walkes.
		Returne, and tell him so: we know the worst.
	Bastard	What ere you thinke, good words I thinke
		were best.
30	**Salisbury**	Our greefes,[†2] and not our manners reason now.
	Bastard	But there is little reason in your greefe.
		Therefore 'twere reason you had manners now.
	Pembroke	Sir, sir, impatience hath his priviledge.
	Bastard	'Tis true, to hurt his master, no mans [3] else.
35	**Salisbury**	This is the prison: [4] What is he lyes heere?
	Pembroke	Oh death, made proud with pure & princely beuty,
		The earth had not a hole to hide this deede.
	Salisbury	Murther, as hating what himselfe hath done,
		Doth lay it open to urge on revenge.
40	**Bigot**	Or when he doom'd this Beautie to a grave,
		Found it too precious Princely, for a grave.
	Salisbury	Sir Richard,[5] what thinke you? you have beheld,[6]
		Or have you read, or heard, or could you thinke?
		Or do you almost thinke, although you see,
45		That you do see?
		Could thought, without this object
		Forme such another?
		This is the very top,
		The heighth, the Crest: or Crest unto the Crest

▼ [1] Ff/most modern texts = 'thin bestained', one excellent modern gloss = 'sin bestained'

▼ [2] F2/most modern texts = 'Greifes', F1 = 'greefcs'

▼ [3] F2/most modern texts = 'man', F1 = 'mans'

SD [4] most modern texts indicate Salisbury now discovers Arthur's body

N [5] this is one of the few occasions the Bastard is addressed by the personal name associated with his title

▼ [6] F3/most modern texts = 'have you beheld', F1 - 2 = 'you have beheld'

50	Of murthers Armes : this is the bloodiest shame,
	The wildest Savagery, the vildest stroke
	That ever wall-ey'd wrath, or staring rage
	Presented to the teares of soft remorse.

Pembroke
All murthers past, do stand excus'd in this :
55 And this so sole, and so unmatcheable,
Shall give a holinesse, a puritie,
To the yet unbegotten sinne of times ; [1]
And prove a deadly blood-shed, but a jest,
Exampled by this heynous spectacle.

Bastard
60 It is a damned, and a bloody worke,
The gracelesse action of a heavy hand,
If that it be the worke of any hand.

Salisbury
If that it be the worke of any hand?
We had a kinde of light, what would ensue :
65 It is the shamefull worke of Huberts hand,
The practice, and the purpose of the king :
From whose obedience I forbid my soule,
Kneeling before this ruine of sweete life,
And breathing to his breathlesse Excellence
70 The Incense of a Vow, a holy Vow :
Never to taste the pleasures of the world,
Never to be infected with delight,
Nor conversant with Ease, and Idlenesse,
Till I have set a glory to this hand,
75 By giving it the worship of Revenge.

Pembroke {&} Bigot
Our soules religiously confirme thy words.

ENTER HUBERT

Hubert
Lords, I am hot with haste, in seeking you,
Arthur doth live, the king hath sent for you.

Salisbury
Oh he is bold, and blushes not at death,
80 Avant thou hatefull villain, get thee gone.

Hubert	I am no villaine.	**Salisbury**	Must I rob the Law? [2]
Bastard	Your sword is bright sir, put it up againe.		
Salisbury	Not till I sheath it in a murtherers skin.		L 17 · b

L 17 · b : 4. 3. 47 - 80

---

[w][1] Ff/most modern texts = 'sin of times', one modern gloss = 'sins of Time'
[SD][2] most modern texts suggest Salisbury draws his sword

Hubert	Stand backe Lord Salsbury, stand backe I say:
85	By heaven, I thinke my sword's as sharpe as yours.
	I would not have you (Lord) forget your selfe,
	Nor tempt the danger of my true defence;
	Least I, by marking of your rage, forget
[1]	your Worth, your Greatnesse, and Nobility.
90 **Bigot**	Out dunghill: dar'st thou brave a Nobleman?
Hubert	Not for my life: But yet I dare defend
	My innocent life [2] against an Emperor.
Salisbury	Thou art a Murtherer.
Hubert	Do not prove me so:
95	Yet I am none.
	Whose tongue so ere speakes false,
	Not truely speakes: who speakes not truly, Lies.
Pembroke	Cut him to peeces.
Bastard	[3] Keepe the peace, I say.
100 **Salisbury**	Stand by, or I shall gaul you Faulconbridge.
Bastard	Thou wer't better gaul the divell Salsbury.
	If thou but frowne on me, or stirre thy foote,
	Or teach thy hastie spleene to do me shame,
	Ile strike thee dead.
105	Put up thy sword betime,
	Or Ile so maule you, and your tosting [4]-Iron,
	That you shall thinke the divell is come from hell.
Bigot	What wilt thou do, renowned Faulconbridge?
	Second a Villaine, and a Murtherer?
110 **Hubert**	Lord Bigot, I am none.
Bigot	Who kill'd this Prince?
Hubert	'Tis not an houre since I left him well:
	I honour'd him, I lov'd him, and will weepe
	My date of life out, for his sweete lives losse.

VP [1] F2/most modern texts set the capital-letter 'Your', signifying the start of a new verse line: F1 sets the lower-case prose indicator 'your'

W [2] Ff/most modern texts = 'life', glosses include 'self' and 'name'

SD [3] most modern texts suggest the Bastard now draws his sword

W [4] Ff = 'tosting', which most modern texts set as 'toasting'

115	**Salisbury**	Trust not those cunning waters of his eyes,
		For villanie is not without such rheume,
		And he, long traded in it, makes it seeme
		Like Rivers of remorse and innocencie.
		Away with me, all you whose soules abhorre
120		Th'uncleanly savours of a Slaughter-house,
		For I am stifled with this smell of sinne.
	Bigot	Away, toward Burie, to the Dolphin there.
	Pembroke	There tel the king, he may inquire us out.

[Ex.{it} Lords]

	Bastard	Here's a good world : knew you of this faire work?
125		Beyond the infinite and boundlesse reach° of mercie,
		(If thou didst this deed of death)° art ÿ¹ damn'd Hubert. °²
	Hubert	Do but heare me sir.
	Bastard	Ha?
		Ile tell thee what.
130		Thou'rt damn'd as blacke, nay nothing is so blacke,
		Thou art more deepe damn'd then Prince Lucifer :
		There is not yet so ugly a fiend of hell
		As thou shalt be, if thou didst kill this childe.
	Hubert	Upon my soule.
135	**Bastard**	If thou didst but consent
		To this most cruell Act : ³ do but dispaire,
		And if thou want'st a Cord, the smallest thred
		That ever Spider twisted from her wombe
		Will serve to strangle thee : A rush will be a beame
140		To hang thee on.
		Or wouldst thou drowne thy selfe,
		Put but a little water in a spoone,
		And it shall be as all the Ocean,
		Enough to stifle such a villaine up.
145		I do suspect thee very greevously.

AB¹ F1 = 'ÿ', (printed as such because of lack of column width), F2/most modern texts = 'thou'

LS² Ff set two long lines (13/12 syllables), repeating the loss of control over Arthur's death the Bastard displayed with John earlier (see footnote #3, page 65): most modern texts restructure the passage to three lines, two regular and a third of four syllables, as shown

RCT³ Ff set a colon, emphasising the curse that is to follow: most modern texts replace the colon with a comma

Hubert	If I in act, consent, or sinne of thought,
	Be guiltie of the stealing that sweete breath
	Which was embounded in this beauteous clay,
	Let hell want paines enough to torture me :
150	I left him well.
Bastard	Go, beare him in thine armes :
	I am amaz'd me thinkes, and loose my way
	Among the thornes, and dangers of this world.

R 17 - b

> [1] How easie dost thou take all England up,
> From forth this morcell of dead Royaltie?
>
> The life, the right, and truth of all this Realme
> Is fled to heaven :   and England now is left

To tug and scamble,[2] and to part by th'teeth
The un-owed interest of proud swelling State :
160   Now for the bare-pickt bone of Majesty,
Doth dogged warre bristle his angry crest,
And snarleth in the gentle eye of peace :
Now Powers from home, and discontents at home
Meet in one line :   and vast confusion waites
165   As doth a Raven on a sicke-falne beast,
The iminent decay of wrested pompe.

Now happy he, whose cloake and center[3] can
Hold out this tempest.
                              Beare away that childe,
170   And follow me with speed :   Ile to the King :
A thousand businesses are briefe in[4] hand,
And heaven it selfe doth frowne upon the Land.

[Exit]

---

[1] Ff's ungrammatical punctuation suggests a somewhat disturbed moment for the Bastard: most modern texts set a more rational sequence, viz.

> How easie dost thou take all England up! (or ?)
> From forth this morcell of dead Royaltie,
> The life, the right, and truth of all this Realme
> Is fled to heaven: and England now is left

[2] Ff/most modern texts = 'scamble', one modern text = 'scramble'

[3] Ff = 'center', modern glosses offer words suggestive of a girdle or belt, viz. 'cincture', 'ceinture' or 'centure'

[4] Ff/most modern texts = 'in', one modern gloss = 'at'

Actus Quartus,[1] Scœna prima

ENTER KING JOHN AND PANDOLPH, ATTENDANTS

·King John· [2]	[3]	Thus have I yeelded up into your hand The Circle of my glory. }
Pandulph		Take againe From this my hand, as holding of the Pope Your Soveraigne greatnesse and authoritie.

5

·John·	Now keep your holy word, go meet the French, And from his holinesse use all your power To stop their marches 'fore we are enflam'd : Our discontented Counties doe revolt : Our people quarrell with obedience, Swearing Allegiance, and the love of soule To stranger-bloud, to forren Royalty ; This inundation of mistempred humor, Rests by you onely to be qualified. Then pause not : for the present time's so sicke, That present medcine must be ministred, Or overthrow incureable ensues.

10

15

Pandulph	It was my breath that blew this Tempest up, Upon your stubborne usage of the Pope : But since you are a gentle convertite, My tongue shall hush againe this storme of warre, And make faire weather in your blustring land : On this Ascension day, remember well, Upon your oath of service to the Pope, Goe I to make the French lay downe their Armes.

20

25

[Exit] [4]

ALT/COMP [1] this is the second 'Actus Quartus' as set by F1: see footnote #1, page 54: most modern texts regard this as the start of Act Five, and name it accordingly: the 4* in the line numbering distinguishes this act from the previous Actus Quartus

P [2] fascinatingly, for this one speech, the prefix shifts from the personal 'John' to the now rarely used status prefix of 'King John'

SD [3] most modern texts add a series of directions surrounding the opening of the scene: they usually encompass
    1/ before speaking, John surrenders the crown
    2/ that either before, during, or after the first speech, he kneels
    3/ that Pandulph crowns John once again as he begins his first speech

SD [4] some modern texts suggest all leave but John, others indicate that just Pandulph and his Attendants exit: either way, the weakness of John's situation and his 'confession' will clearly be seen

John	Is this Ascension day? did not the Prophet
	Say, that before Ascension day at noone,
	My Crowne I should give off? even so I have :
	I did suppose it should be on constraint,
30 | | But (heavn be thank'd) it is but voluntary. |

ENTER BASTARD

Bastard	All Kent hath yeelded : nothing there holds out
	But Dover Castle : London hath receiv'd
	Like a kinde Host, the Dolphin and his powers .
	Your Nobles will not heare you, but are gone
35		To offer service to your enemy :
	And wilde amazement hurries up and downe
	The little number of your doubtfull friends .

John	Would not my Lords returne to me againe	
	After they heard yong Arthur was alive?	L 18 - c

40	**Bastard**	They found him dead, and cast into the streets,
	An empty Casket, where the Jewell of life
	By some damn'd hand was rob'd, and tane away .

John	That villaine Hubert told me he did live.

Bastard	So on my soule he did, for ought he knew :
45		But wherefore doe you droope? why looke you sad?
	Be great in act, as you have beene in thought :
	Let not the world see feare and sad distrust
	Governe the motion of a kinglye eye :
	Be stirring as†1 the time, be fire with fire,
50		Threaten the theatner, and out-face the brow
	Of bragging horror : So shall inferior eyes
	That borrow their behaviours from the great,
	Grow great by your example, and put on
	The dauntlesse spirit of resolution .
55		Away, and glister like the god of warre
	When he intendeth to become the field :
	Shew boldnesse and aspiring confidence :
	What, shall they seeke the Lion in his denne,
	And fright him there? and make him tremble there?
60		Oh let it not be said : forrage, and runne
	To meet displeasure farther from the dores,
	And grapple with him ere he come so nye .

▼ 1 F2/most modern texts = 'stirring as', F1 = 'stirringas'

John	The Legat of the Pope hath beene with mee,
	And I have made a happy peace with him,
65	And he hath promis'd to dismisse the Powers
	Led by the Dolphin.

Bastard	Oh inglorious league:
	Shall we upon the footing of our land,
	Send fayre-play-orders, and make comprimise,
70	Insinuation, parley, and base truce
	To Armes Invasive?

Shall a beardlesse boy,
A cockred-silken wanton brave our fields,
And flesh his spirit in a warre-like soyle,
75 Mocking the ayre with colours idlely spred,
And finde no checke?

Let us my Liege to Armes:
Perchance the Cardinall cannot make your peace;
Or if he doe, let it at least be said
80 They saw we had a purpose of defence.

John	Have thou the ordering of this present time.
Bastard	Away then with good courage: ¹ yet I know
	Our Partie may well meet a prowder foe.

[Exeunt]

SD/A ₁ most modern texts either have John now exit, or suggest the remainder of this speech is spoken as an aside

Scœna Secunda

ENTER (IN ARMES) DOLPHIN, SALISBURY, MELOONE, PEM-
BROKE, BIGOT, SOULDIERS

Dolphin	My Lord Melloone, let this be coppied out,
	And keepe it safe for our remembrance :
	Returne the president to those Lords againe,
	That having our faire order written downe,
5	Both they and we, perusing ore these notes
	May know wherefore we tooke the Sacrament,
	And keepe our faithes firme and inviolable.
Salisbury	Upon our sides it never shall be broken.
	And Noble Dolphin, albeit we sweare
10	A voluntary zeale, and an un-urg'd Faith
	To your proceedings : yet beleeve me Prince,
	I am not glad that such a sore of Time
	Should seeke a plaster by contemn'd revolt,
	And heale the inveterate Canker of one wound,
15	By making many : Oh it grieves my soule,
	That I must draw this mettle ¹ from my side
	To be a widdow-maker : oh, and there
	Where honourable rescue, and defence
	Cries out upon the name of Salisbury.
20	But such is the infection of the time,
	That for the health and Physicke of our right,
	We cannot deale but with the very hand
	Of sterne Injustice, and confused wrong :
	And is't not pitty, (oh my grieved friends)
25	That we, the sonnes and children of this Isle,
	Was borne to see so sad an houre as this,
	Wherein we step after a stranger, march
	Upon her gentle bosom, and fill up
	Her Enemies rankes?
30	I must withdraw, and weepe
	Upon the spot of this inforced cause,
	To grace the Gentry of a Land remote,
	And follow unacquainted colours heere :

R 18 - c

R 18 - c / L 19 - c : 5. 2. 1 - 32

▼ ¹ Ff = 'mettle', some modern texts set 'metal' thus reducing the power of Salisbury's image

What heere?
　　　　　　　O Nation that thou couldst remove,
35
That Neptunes Armes who clippeth thee about,
Would beare thee from the knowledge of thy selfe,
And cripple [1] thee unto a Pagan shore,
Where these two Christian Armies might combine
40
The bloud of malice, in a vaine of league,
And not to spend it so un-neighbourly.

Dolphin　　A noble temper dost thou shew in this,
And great affections wrastling in thy bosome
Doth make an earth-quake of Nobility:
45
Oh, what a noble combat hast [2] fought
Between compulsion, and a brave respect:
Let me wipe off this honourable dewe,
That silverly doth progresse on thy cheekes:
My heart hath melted at a Ladies teares,
50
Being an ordinary Inundation:
But this effusion of such manly drops,
This showre, blowne up by tempest of the soule,
Startles mine eyes, and makes me more amaz'd
Then had I seene the vaultie top of heaven
55
Figur'd quite ore with†[3] burning Meteors.

Lift up thy brow (renowned Salisburie)
And with a great heart heave away this storme:
Commend these waters to those baby-eyes
That never saw the giant-world [4] enrag'd,
60
Nor met with Fortune, other then at feasts,
Full warm of blood, of mirth, of gossipping:
Come, come; for thou shalt thrust thy hand as deepe
Into the purse of rich prosperity
As Lewis himselfe: so (Nobles) shall you all,
65
That knit your sinewes to the strength of mine.

ENTER PANDULPHO [5]

▼ [1] Ff = 'cripple', most modern texts = 'grapple'

▼ [2] F 1- 3 set a nine syllable line: F4/most modern texts add 'thou'

▼ [3] F2/most modern texts set = 'with', F1 = 'wirh'

▼ [4] more than in any other play, many texts have sought to join two Ff words together by adding a connecting hyphen where none originally existed, so as to create a compound epithet (see the specific Introduction to this play): surprisingly both here, 'giant-world' and in the previous line 'baby-eyes', where Ff finally do set hyphens (admittedly not for compound-epithets) most modern texts omit them

N/SD [5] most modern texts set the spelling usually used for the legate's name, 'Pandulph': most texts add he is attended, and some delay the entry one line: one commentator suggests adding the sound of a trumpet to give rise to the image of 'methinkes an Angell spake'

And even there, methinkes an Angell spake,
Looke where the holy Legate comes apace,
To give us warrant from the hand of heaven,
And on our actions set the name of right
70   With holy breath.
                              }

Pandulph   Haile noble Prince of France:
The next is this: King John hath reconcil'd
Himselfe to Rome, his spirit is come in,
That so stood out against the holy Church,
75   The great Metropolis and Sea [1] of Rome:
Therefore thy threatning Colours now winde up,
And tame the savage spirit of wilde warre,
That like a Lion fostered up at hand,
It may lie gently at the foot of peace,
80   And be no further harmefull then in shewe.

Dolphin   Your Grace shall pardon me, I will not backe: L 19 - c
I am too high-borne to be proportied [2]
To be a secondary at controll,
Or usefull serving-man, and Instrument
85   To any Soveraigne State throughout the world.

Your breath first kindled the dead coale of warres,
Betweene this chastiz'd kingdome and my selfe,
And brought in matter that should feed this fire;
And now 'tis farre too huge to be blowne out
90   With that same weake winde, which enkindled it:
You taught me how to know the face of right,
Acquainted me with interest to this Land,
Yea, thrust this enterprize into my heart,
And come ye now to tell me John hath made
95   His peace with Rome?   what is that peace to me?

I (by the honour of my marriage bed)
After yong Arthur, claime this Land for mine,
And now it is halfe conquer'd, must I backe,
Because that John hath made his peace with Rome?
100   Am I Romes slave?
                    What penny hath Rome borne?

What men provided?
                  What munition sent
To under-prop this Action?

L 19 - c / R 19 - c : 5. 2. 63 - 99

^W [1] F4/most modern texts = 'see', F1 - 3 = 'Sea'

^{W/PCT} [2] F1 = 'proportied': most modern texts set F2's 'propertied' and add F4's comma

105		Is't not I
	That under-goe this charge?	
		Who else but I,
	And such as to my claime are liable,	
	Sweat in this businesse, and maintaine this warre?	

110   Have I not heard these Islanders shout out
Vive le Roy, as I have bank'd their Townes?

Have I not heere the best Cards for the game
To winne this easie match, plaid for a Crowne?

And shall I now give ore the yeelded Set?

115   No, no,[1] on my soule it never shall be said.

Pandulph   You looke but on the out-side of this worke.

Dolphin   Out-side or in-side, I will not returne
Till my attempt so much be glorified,
As to my ample hope was promised,

120   Before I drew this gallant head of warre,
And cull'd these fiery spirits from the world
To out looke Conquest, and to winne renowne
Even in the jawes of danger, and of death :   [2]
What lusty Trumpet thus doth summon us?

ENTER BASTARD

125   **Bastard**   According to the faire-play of the world,
Let me have audience :   I am sent to speake :
My holy Lord of Millane, from the King
I come to learne how you have dealt for him :
And, as you answer, I doe know the scope

130   And warrant limited unto my tongue.

Pandulph   The Dolphin is too wilfull opposite
And will not temporize with my intreaties :
He flatly saies, hee ll[3] not lay downe his Armes.

Bastard   By all the bloud that ever fury breath'd,
135   The youth saies well.
                   Now heare our English King,
For thus his Royaltie doth speake in me :

▼ 1   since Ff set an eleven syllable line, metrically minded commentators suggest dropping the second 'no', despite its oratorical, emphatic value

SD 2   because of the next line most modern texts set a direction for an off-stage trumpet

▼ 3   F2/most modern texts = 'hee'll', F1 = 'hee ll'

He is prepar'd, and reason to he should,
This apish and unmannerly approach,
140   This harness'd Maske, and unadvised Revell,
This un-heard [1] sawcinesse and boyish Troopes,
The King doth smile at, and is well prepar'd
To whip this dwarfish warre, this Pigmy Armes
From out the circle of his Territories.

145   That hand which had the strength, even at your dore,
To cudgell you, and make you take the hatch,
To dive like Buckets in concealed Welles,
To crowch in litter of your stable planckes,
To lye like pawnes, lock'd up in chests and truncks,
150   To hug with swine, to seeke sweet safety out
In vaults and prisons, and to thrill and shake,   R 19 - c
Even at the crying of your Nations crow,
Thinking this [2] voyce an armed Englishman.

Shall that victorious hand be feebled heere,
155   That in your Chambers gave you chasticement?

No :   know the gallant Monarch is in Armes,
And like an Eagle, o're his ayerie towres,
To sowsse annoyance that comes neere his Nest ;
And you degenerate, you ingrate Revolts,
160   [3] you bloudy Nero's, ripping up the wombe
Of your deere Mother-England :   blush for shame :
For your owne Ladies, and pale-visag'd Maides,
Like Amazons, come tripping after drummes :
Their thimbles into armed Gantlets change,
165   Their Needl's to Lances, and their gentle hearts
To fierce and bloody inclination.

Dolphin   There end thy brave, and turn thy face in peace,
We grant thou canst out-scold us :   Far thee well,
We hold our time too precious to be spent
170   With such a brabler.

Pandulph   Give me leave to speake.
                                                         }
Bastard   No, I will speake.
                                                         }
Dolphin   We will attend to neyther :

---

[1] Ff = 'un-heard', most modern texts set 'inhaired'

[2] Ff/most modern texts = 'this', one modern gloss = 'his'

[3] F1 sets the lower case 'you', suggesting prose: F2/most modern texts set the upper-case 'You', continuing
the verse of scene and speech

75		Strike up the drummes, and let the tongue of warre Pleade for our interest, and our being heere.
	Bastard	Indeede your drums being beaten, wil cry out; And so shall you, being beaten: Do but start An eccho with the clamor of thy drumme, And even at hand, a drumme is readie brac'd,
80		That shall reverberate all, as lowd as thine.
		Sound but another, and another shall (As lowd as thine) rattle the Welkins eare, And mocke the deepe mouth'd Thunder: for at hand (Not trusting to this halting Legate†1 heere,
85		Whom he hath us'd rather for sport, then neede) Is warlike John: and in his fore-head sits A bare-rib'd death, whose office is this day To feast upon whole thousands of the French.
	Dolphin	Strike up our drummes, to finde this danger out.
90	**Bastard**	And thou shalt finde it (Dolphin) do not doubt ²

[Exeunt]

L 20 - b : 5. 2. 164 - 180

▼ 1 F2/most modern texts = 'Legate', F1 = 'Lcgate'

RCT 2 F1 - 2 set no punctuation, perhaps suggesting the exit and/or call for Alarums starting the next scene cut
into the last words: F3/most modern texts set a period

Scæna Tertia

ALARUMS. ENTER JOHN AND HUBERT

John	How goes the day with us? oh tell me Hubert.
Hubert	Badly I feare : how fares your Majesty?
John	This Feaver that hath troubled me so long, Lyes heavie on me : oh, my heart is sicke.

ENTER A MESSENGER

5   **Messenger**   My Lord :   your valiant kinsman Falconbridge,
Desires your Majestie to leave the field,
And send him word by me, which way you go.

       John   Tell him toward Swinsted,[1] to the Abbey there.

       Messenger   Be of good comfort :   for the [2] great supply
10   That was expected by the Dolphin heere,
Are wrack'd three nights ago on Goodwin sands.

                      This newes was brought to Richard but even now,[3]
The French fight coldly, and retyre themselves.

       John   Aye me, this tyrant Feaver burnes mee up,
15   And will not let me welcome this good newes.

                      Set on toward Swinsted :   to my Litter straight,
Weaknesse possesseth me, and I am faint.

[Exeunt]

L 20 - b

---

[1] as most commentators point out, Ff were historically mistaken in setting 'Swinsted' since it had no Abbey: at least one modern text sets the correct location 'Swineshead'

[2] F2/most modern texts = 'the', F1 = 'rhe'

[3] Ff set a comma, establishing a rush for the Messenger (eagerness? out of breath?) as he slips from one idea to the next: most modern texts replace the comma with a period

Scena Quarta

ENTER SALISBURY, PEMBROKE, AND BIGOT

Salisbury	I did not thinke the King so stor'd with friends.
Pembroke	Up once againe : put spirit in the French, If they miscarry : ¹ we miscarry too.
Salisbury	That misbegotten divell Falconbridge, In spight of spight, alone upholds the day.
Pembroke	They say King John sore sick, hath left the field.

ENTER MELOON WOUNDED ²

Meloon	Lead me to the Revolts of England heere.
Salisbury	When we were happie, we had other names.
Pembroke	It is the Count Meloone.
Salisbury	Wounded to death.
Meloon	Fly Noble English, you are bought and sold, Unthred the rude eye of Rebellion, And welcome home againe discarded faith, Seeke out King John, and fall before his feete : For if the French be Lords ³ of this loud day, He meanes to recompence the paines you take, By cutting off your heads : Thus hath he sworne, And I with him, and many moe with mee, Upon the Altar at S. ⁴ Edmondsbury, Even on that Altar, where we swore to you Deere Amity, and everlasting love.
Salisbury	May this be possible? May this be true?

5

10

15

20

[PCT] ¹ F1 - 2 emphasise the desperate situation of the English 'rebels' by setting a rhetorical colon: F3/most modern texts set a comma, and sometimes replace the comma at the end of the previous line with a period

[SD] ² some modern texts suggest he is led in by Soldiers (whether French or English is not specified)

[W] ³ since 'He' starts the following line, one commentator suggests altering Ff/most modern texts' phrase 'if the French be Lords' to 'if he be Lord', while another commentator suggests altering 'He' to 'Lewis'

[AB] ⁴ F2/most modern texts = 'Saint', F1 sets the abbreviation 'S.'

Meloon
Have I not hideous death within my view,
Retaining but a quantity of life,
Which bleeds away, even as a forme of waxe
Resolveth from his figure 'gainst the fire?

What in the world should make me now deceive,
Since I must loose the use of all deceite?
Why should I then be false, since it is true
That I must dye heere, and live hence, by Truth?

I say againe, if Lewis do win the day,
He is forsworne, if ere those eyes of yours
Behold another day breake in the East:
But even this night, whose blacke contagious breath
Already smoakes about the burning Crest
Of the old, feeble, and day-wearied Sunne,
Even this ill night, your breathing shall expire,
Paying the fine of rated Treachery,
Even with a treacherous fine of all your lives:
If Lewis, by your assistance win the day.

Commend me to one Hubert, with your King;
The love of him, and this respect besides
(For that my Grandsire was an Englishman)
Awakes my Conscience to confesse all this.

In lieu whereof, I pray you beare me hence
From forth the noise and rumour of the Field;
Where I may thinke the remnant of my thoughts
In peace: and part this bodie and my soule
With contemplation, and devout desires.

Salisbury
We do beleeve thee, and beshrew my soule,
But I do love the favour, and the forme
Of this most faire occasion, by the which
We will untread the steps of damned flight,
And like a bated and retired Flood,
Leaving our ranknesse and irregular course,
Stoope lowe within those bounds we have ore-look'd,
And calmly run on in obedience
Even to our Ocean, to our great King John.
My arme shall give thee helpe to beare thee hence, R 20 - b
For I do see the cruell pangs of death
Right [1] in thine eye.
                    Away, my friends, new flight,
And happie newnesse, that intends old right.
                    [Exeunt] [2]

W[1] Ff = 'Right', modern glosses include 'Fight' and 'Bright'
SD[2] most modern texts indicate they take off the dead/dying Meloon

Scena Quinta

ENTER DOLPHIN, AND HIS TRAINE

Dolphin	The Sun of heaven (me thought) was loth to set;
	But staid, and made the Westerne Welkin blush,
	When English measure backward their owne ground
	In faint Retire: Oh bravely came we off,
	When with a volley of our needlesse shot,
	After such bloody toile, we bid good night,
	And woon'd our tott'ring [1] colours clearly up,
	Last in the field, and almost Lords of it.

5

ENTER A MESSENGER

Messenger	Where is my Prince, the Dolphin?
	⟩
Dolphin	Heere: what newes?

10

Messenger	The Count Meloone is slaine: The English Lords
	By his perswasion, are againe falne off,
	And your supply, which you have wish'd so long,
	Are cast away, and sunke on Goodwin sands.

Dolphin	Ah fowle, shrew'd newes.
	Beshrew thy very hart:
	I did not thinke to be so sad to night
	As this hath made me.
	Who was he that said
	King John did flie an houre or two before
	The stumbling night did part our wearie powres?

15

20

Messenger	Who ever spoke it, it is true my Lord.

Dolphin	Well: keepe good quarter, & good care to night,
	The day shall not be up so soone as I,
	To try the faire adventure of to morrow.

25

[Exeunt]

L 21 - b : 5. 5. 1 - 22

▼ [1] Ff = 'woon'd our tott'ring colours' which various modern texts suggest emending to 'wound our tatter'd colours'

Scena Sexta

ENTER BASTARD AND HUBERT, SEVERALLY

Hubert	Whose there? Speake hoa, speake quickely, or I shoote.
Bastard	A Friend. What art thou?
Hubert	Of the part of England.
Bastard	Whether doest thou go?
Hubert	What's that to thee? ¹ Why may not I demand of thine affaires, As well as thou of mine?
Bastard	Hubert, I thinke.
Hubert	Thou hast a perfect thought: I will upon all hazards well beleeve Thou art my friend, that know'st my tongue so well: Who art thou?
Bastard	Who thou wilt: and if thou please Thou maist be-friend me so much, as to thinke I come one way of the Plantagenets.
Hubert	Unkinde remembrance: thou, & endles ² night, Have done me shame: Brave Soldier, pardon me, That any accent breaking from thy tongue, Should scape the true acquaintance of mine eare.
Bastard	Come, come: sans complement, What newes abroad?

Line numbers: 5, 10, 15, 20

L 21 - b : 5. 6. 1 - 16

ALT/LS ¹ though the passage works well as set, there has been much discussion of the opening six lines (up to the point Hubert and the Bastard recognise each other): commentators offer wholesale revisions of the line assignments (see *The New Cambridge Shakespeare King John*, op. cit., pages 186 - 8, for a detailed discussion); the least invasive alteration is that some modern texts take this and the following line from Hubert and add them to the Bastard's following speech

² Ff = 'endles', some modern texts = 'eyeless'

25	Hubert	Why heere walke I, in the black brow of night To finde you out.

	Bastard	Briefe[†1] then : and what's the newes?
	Hubert	O my sweet sir, newes fitting to the night, Blacke, fearefull, comfortlesse, and horrible.
30	Bastard	Shew me the very wound of this ill newes, I am no woman, Ile not swound at it.
	Hubert	The King I feare is poyson'd by a Monke, I left him almost speechlesse, and broke out To acquaint you with this evill, that you might The better arme you to the sodaine time, Then if you had at leisure knowne of this.
35		
	Bastard	How did he take it? Who did taste to him?
	Hubert	A Monke I tell you, a resolved villaine Whose Bowels sodainly burst out : The King Yet speakes, and peradventure may recover.
40		
	Bastard	Who didst thou leave to tend his Majesty?

	Hubert	Why know you not?
		            The Lords are all come
		      backe,
		And brought Prince Henry in their companie,
		At whose request the king hath pardon'd them,
		And they are all about his Majestie.

45		
	Bastard	With-hold thine indignation, mighty heaven, And tempt us not to beare above our power.
50		
		Ile tell thee Hubert, halfe my power this night Passing these Flats, are taken by the Tide, These Lincolne-Washes have devoured them, My selfe, well mounted, hardly have escap'd.
55		Away before : Conduct me to the king, I doubt he will be dead, or ere I come.

[Exeunt]

▼ 1 F2/most modern texts = 'Briefe', F1 = 'Brcfe'

Scena Septima

ENTER PRINCE HENRY, SALISBURIE, AND BIGOT

Henry	It is too late, the life of all his blood
	Is touch'd, corruptibly: and his pure braine
	(Which some suppose the soules fraile dwelling house)
	Doth by the idle Comments that it makes,
5	Fore-tell the ending of mortality.

ENTER PEMBROKE

Pembroke	His Highnesse yet doth speak, & holds beleefe,
	That being brought into the open ayre,
	It would allay the burning qualitie
	Of that fell poison which assayleth him.
10 **Henry**	Let him be brought into the Orchard heere: [1]
	Doth he still rage?
Pembroke	He is more patient
	Then when you left him; even now he sung.
Henry	Oh vanity of sicknesse: fierce extreames
15	In their continuance, will not feele themselves.
	Death having praide upon the outward parts
	Leaves them invisible,[2] and his seige is now
	Against the winde,[3] the which he prickes and wounds
	With many legions of strange fantasies,
20	Which in their throng, and presse to that last hold,
	Counfound themselves.
	'Tis strange ÿ[4] death shold sing:
	I am the Symet[5] to this pale faint Swan,
	Who chaunts a dolefull hymne to his owne death,
25	And from the organ-pipe of frailety sings
	His soule and body to their lasting rest.

SD 1 since Salisbury and Pembroke have dialogue before John is brought in, most modern texts suggest Bigot exits to get the King

W 2 Ff = 'invisible', most modern texts = 'insensible'

W 3 Ff = 'winde', some modern texts = 'mind'

AB 4 F1 = 'ÿ', (printed as such because of lack of column width), F2/most modern texts = 'that'

W 5 Ff = 'Symet', most modern texts = 'cygnet'

Salisbury	Be of good comfort (Prince) for you are borne To set a forme upon that indigest Which he hath left so shapelesse, and so rude.	

JOHN BROUGHT IN [1]

30	**John**	I marrie, now my soule hath elbow roome, R 21 - b It would not out at windowes, nor at doores, There is so hot a summer in my bosome, That all my bowels crumble up to dust: I am a scribled forme drawne with a pen Upon a Parchment, and against this fire Do I shrinke up.
35		

Henry	How fares your Majesty?
John	Poyson'd, ill fare: [2] dead, forsooke, cast off, And none of you will bid the winter come To thrust his ycie fingers in my maw; Nor let my kingdomes Rivers take their course Through my burn'd bosome: nor intreat the North To make his bleake windes kisse my parched lips, And comfort me with cold. I do not aske you much, I begge cold comfort: and you are so straight And so ingratefull, you deny me that.

Henry	Oh that there were some vertue in my teares, That might releeve you.
John	The salt in them is hot. Within me is a hell, and there the poyson Is, as a fiend, confin'd to tyrannize, On unrepreevable condemned blood.

ENTER BASTARD [3]

Bastard	Oh, I am scalded with my violent motion And spleene of speede, to see your Majesty.
John	Oh Cozen, thou art come to set mine eye:

(Line numbers in left margin: 40, 45, 50, 55)

R 21 - b / L 22 - b : 5. 7. 25 - 51

SD [1] those modern texts suggesting Bagot went to get John now suggest he supervises John's bringing in: at least one text suggests John is brought in on a litter

W [2] Ff = 'ill fare', one modern gloss = 'ill fate'

SD [3] at least one commentator suggests Hubert accompanies him

91

The tackle of my heart, is crack'd and burnt,
And all the shrowds wherewith my life should saile,
Are turned to one thred, one little haire:
60   My heart hath one poore string to stay it by,
Which holds but till thy newes be uttered,
And then all this thou seest, is but a clod,
And module of confounded royalty.

Bastard   The Dolphin is preparing hither-ward,
65   Where heaven [1] he knowes how we shall answer him.

For in a night the best part of my powre,
As I upon advantage did remove,
Were in the Washes all unwarily,
Devoured by the unexpected flood. [2]

70 **Salisbury**   You breath these dead newes in as dead an eare [3]
My Liege, my Lord: but now a King, now thus.

Henry   Even so must I run on, and even so stop.

What surety of the world, what hope, what stay,
When this was now a King, and now is clay?

75 **Bastard**   Art thou gone so?
                I do but stay behinde,
To do the office for thee, of revenge,
And then my soule shall waite on thee to heaven,   L 22 - b
As it on earth hath bene thy servant still.

80   Now, now you Starres, that move in your right spheres,
Where be your powres?
                    Shew now your mended faiths,
And instantly returne with me againe. [4]

To push destruction, and perpetuall shame
85   Out of the weake doore of our fainting Land:
Straight let us seeke, or straight we shall be sought,
The Dolphine rages at our verie heeles.

W [1] Ff = 'heaven', some modern texts = 'God'

SD [2] as the ensuing dialogue indicates, most modern texts suggest John now dies

PCT [3] probably through lack of column width F1 - 3 set no punctuation - perhaps suggesting Salisbury's emotions get the better of him and he plunges on: F4/most modern texts set a period

PCT [4] F1 sets an ungrammatical period, as if the Bastard needs a moment before he can continue: F2/most modern texts set a comma

Salisbury	It seemes you know not then so much as we,
	The Cardinall Pandulph is within at rest,
90	Who halfe an houre since came from the Dolphin,
	And brings from him such offers of our peace,
	As we with honor and respect may take,
	With purpose presently to leave this warre.

Bastard He will the rather do it, when he sees
95 Our selves well sinew'd [1] to our defence.

Salisbury Nay, 'tis in a manner done already,
For many carriages hee hath dispatch'd
To the sea side, and put his cause and quarrell
To the disposing of the Cardinall,
100 With whom your selfe, my selfe, and other Lords,
If you thinke meete, this afternoone will poast
To consummate this businesse happily.

Bastard Let it be so, and you my noble Prince,
With other Princes that may best be spar'd,
105 Shall waite upon your Fathers Funerall.

Henry At Worster must his bodie be interr'd,
For so he will'd it.

Bastard Thither shall it then,
And happily may your sweet selfe put on
110 The lineall state, and glorie of the Land,
To whom with all submission on my knee,
I do bequeath my faithfull services
And true subjection everlastingly. [2]

Salisbury And the like tender of our love wee make
115 To rest without a spot for evermore.

Henry I have a kinde soule, that would give thankes,
And knowes†[3] not how to do it, but with teares.

R 22 - b : 5. 7. 81 - 109

[w] [1] since Ff set a nine syllable line, metrically minded modern texts either expand Ff's 'sinew'd' to 'sinewed' or set 'sinew'd to our own defence'

[SD] [2] from the dialogue, most modern texts suggest the Bastard kneels during or after his speech, and the Lords do likewise during or after the next

[w] [3] F2/most modern texts = 'knowes', F1 = 'kno wes'

Bastard   ¹ Oh let us pay the time : ² but needfull woe,
Since it hath beene before hand with our greefes.

▌20   This England never did, nor never shall
Lye at the proud foote of a Conqueror,
But when it first did helpe to wound it selfe.

Now, these her Princes are come home againe,
Come the three corners of the world in Armes,
▌25   And we shall shocke them :   Naught shall make us rue,
If England to it selfe, do rest but true.

[Exeunt]

R 22 - b

3

R 22 - b : 5. 7. 110 - 118

ˢᴰ ₁ most modern texts suggest the Bastard now rises

ᴾᶜᵀ ₂ Ff set an unusual colon, presumably highlighting what comes after, explaining how time should be paid, i.e. with 'needfull woe': most modern texts omit the punctuation

ᶜᵒᵐᵖ ₃ perhaps because of spacing, F1 sets just a decorative ending without the word FINIS used to end most plays

APPENDIX A
THE UNEASY RELATIONSHIP OF FOLIO,
QUARTOS, AND MODERN TEXTS

Between the years 1590 and 1611, one William Shakespeare, a playwright and
or, delivered to the company of which he was a major shareholder at least thirty-
en plays in handwritten manuscript form. Since the texts belonged to the com-
y upon delivery, he derived no extra income from publishing them. Indeed, as
as scholars can establish, he took no interest in the publication of his plays.

Consequently, without his supervision, yet during his lifetime and shortly after,
eral different publishers printed eighteen of these plays, each in separate edi-
ns. Each of these texts, known as **'Quartos'** because of the page size and method
folding each printed sheet, was about the size of a modern hardback novel. In
3, seven years after Shakespeare's death, Heminges and Condell, two friends,
atrical colleagues, actors, and fellow shareholders in the company, passed on to
printer, William Jaggard, the handwritten copies of not only these eighteen plays
a further eighteen, of which seventeen had been performed but not yet seen in
nt.[1] These thirty-six plays were issued in one large volume, each page about the
of a modern legal piece of paper. Anything printed in this larger format was
wn as 'folio', again because of the page size and the method of sheet folding.
us the 1623 printing of the collected works is known as **the First Folio,** its 1632
rint (with more than 1600 unauthorised corrections) the Second Folio, and the
t reprint, the 1666 Third Folio, added the one missing play, *Pericles* (which had
n set in quarto and performed).

The handwritten manuscript used for the copies of the texts from which both
artos and the First Folio were printed came from a variety of sources. Closest to
kespeare were those in his own hand, known as the 'foul papers' because of the
ural blottings, crossings out, and corrections. Sometimes he had time to pass the
terial on to a manuscript copyist who would make a clean copy, known as the 'fair
ers'. Whether fair (if there was sufficient time) or foul (if the performance dead-
was close), the papers would be passed on to the Playhouse, where a 'Playhouse
y' would be made, from which the 'sides' (individual copies of each part with just
ngle cue line) would be prepared for each actor. Whether Playhouse copy, fair pa-
s, or foul, the various Elizabethan and Jacobean handwritten manuscripts from
ich the quartos and Folio came have long since disappeared.

The first printed texts of the Shakespeare plays were products of a speaking-
aring society. They were based on rhetoric, a verbal form of arranging logic and ar-

---

Though written between 1605–09, *Timon of Athens* was not performed publicly until 1761.

gument in a persuasive, pleasing, and entertaining fashion so as to win personal and public debates, a system which allowed individuals to express at one and the same time the steppingstones in an argument while releasing the underlying emotional feelings that accompanied it.[2] Naturally, when ideas were set on paper they mirrored this same form of progression in argument and the accompanying personal release allowing both neat and untidy thoughts to be seen at a glance (see the General Introduction, pp. xvi–xxi). Thus what was set on paper was not just a silent debate. It was at the same time a reminder of how the human voice might be heard both logically and passionately in that debate.

Such reminders did not last into the eighteenth century. Three separate but interrelated needs insisted on cleaning up the original printings so that silent and speaking reader alike could more easily appreciate the beauties of one of England's greatest geniuses.

First, by 1700, publishing's main thrust was to provide texts to be read privately by people of taste and learning. Since grammar was now the foundation for all writing, publication, and reading, all the Elizabethan and early Jacobean material still based on rhetoric appeared at best archaic and at worst incomprehensible. All printing followed the new universality of grammatical and syntactical standards, standards which still apply today. Consequently any earlier book printed prior to the establishment of these standards had to be reshaped in order to be understood. And the Folio/Quarto scripts, even the revamped versions which had already begun to appear, presented problems in this regard, especially when dealing in the moments of messy human behaviour. Thus, while the first texts were reshaped according to the grammatical knowledge of the 1700s, much of the shaping of the rhetoric was (inadvertently) removed from the plays.

Secondly, the more Shakespeare came to be recognized as a literary poet rather than as a theatrical genius, the less the plays were likely to be considered as performance texts. Indeed plot lines of several of his plays were altered (or ignored) to satisfy the more refined tastes of the period. And the resultant demands for poetic and literary clarity, as well as those of grammar, altered the first printings even further.

Thirdly, scholars argued a need for revision of both Quarto and Folio texts because of 'interfering hands' (hands other than Shakespeare's) having had undue influence on the texts. No matter whether foul or fair papers or Playhouse copy, so the argument ran, several intermediaries would be involved between Shakespeare's writing of the plays and the printing of them. If the fair papers provided the source text

---

[2] For an extraordinarily full analysis of the art of rhetoric, readers are guided to Sister Miriam Joseph, *Shakespeare's Use of the Arts of Language* (New York: Haffner Publishing Co., 1947) For a more theatrical overview, readers are directed to Bertram Joseph, *Acting Shakespeare* (New York: Theatre Arts Books, 1960). For an overview involving aspects of Ff/Qq, readers are immodestly recommended to Neil Freeman, *Shakespeare's First Texts*, op. cit.

copyist might add some peculiarities, as per the well documented Ralph Crane.[3] If the Playhouse copy was the source text, extra information, mainly stage directions, would have been added by someone other than Shakespeare, turning the play from somewhat literary document into a performance text. Finally, while more than five different compositors were involved in setting the First Folio, five did the bulk of the printing house work: each would have their individual pattern of typesetting — compositor E being singled out as far weaker than the rest. Thus between Shakespeare and the printed text might lie the hand(s) of as few as one and as many as three other people, even more when more than one compositor set an individual play. Therefore critics argue because there is the chance of so much interference between Shakespearean intent and the first printings of the plays, the plays do not offer a stylistic whole, i.e., while the words themselves are less likely to be interfered with, their shapings, the material consistently altered in the early 1700s, are not that of a single hand, and thus cannot be relied upon.

These well-intentioned grammatical and poetic alterations may have introduced Shakespeare to a wider reading audience, but their unforeseen effect was to remove the Elizabethan flavour of argument and of character development (especially in the areas of stress and the resulting textual irregularities), thus watering down and removing literally thousands of rhetorical and theatrical clues that those first performance scripts contained. And it is from this period that the division between ancient and modern texts begins. As a gross generalisation, the first texts, the First Folio and the quartos, could be dubbed 'Shakespeare for the stage'; the second, revamped early 1700 texts 'Shakespeare for the page'.

And virtually all current editions are based on the page texts of the early 1700s. While the words of each play remain basically the same, what shapes them, their sentences, punctuation, spelling, capitalisation and sometimes even line structure, is often altered, unwittingly destroying much of their practical theatrical value.

It is important to neither condemn the modern editions nor blindly accept the authority of the early stage texts as gospel. This is not a case of 'old texts good, so modern texts bad'. The modern texts are of great help in literary and historical research, especially as to the meanings of obscure words and phrases, and in explaining literary allusions and historical events. They offer guidance to alternative text readings made by reputed editors, plus sound grammatical readings of difficult passages and clarification of errors that appear in the first printings.[4] In short, they can

---

Though not of the theatre (his principle work was to copy material for lawyers) Crane was involved in the preparation of at least five plays in the Folio, as well as two plays for Thomas Middleton. Scholars characterise his work as demonstrating regular and careful scene and act division, though he is criticised for his heavy use of punctuation and parentheses, apostrophes and hyphens, and 'massed entry' stage directions, i.e. where all the characters with entrances in the scene are listed in a single direction at the top of the scene irrespective of where they are supposed to enter.

give the starting point of the play's journey, an understanding of the story, and the conflict between characters within the story. But they can only go so far.

They cannot give you fully the conflict within each character, the very essence for the fullest understanding of the development and resolution of any Shakespeare play. Thanks to their rhetorical, theatrical base the old texts add this vital extra element. They illustrate with great clarity the 'ever-changing present' (see p. xvi in the General Introduction) in the intellectual and emotional life of each character; their passages of harmony and dysfunction, and transitions between such passages; the moments of their personal costs or rewards; and their sensual verbal dance of debate and release. In short, the old texts clearly demonstrate the essential elements of living, breathing, reacting humanity—especially in times of joyous or painful stress.

By presenting the information contained in the First Folio, together with modern restructurings, both tested against theatrical possibilities, these texts should go far in bridging the gap between the two different points of view.

---

[4] For example, the peculiar phrase 'a Table of greene fields' assigned to Mistress Quickly in describing the death of Falstaffe, *Henry V* (Act Two, Scene 3), has been superbly diagnosed as a case of poor penmanship being badly transcribed: the modern texts wisely set 'a babbled of green fields' instead.

NEIL FREEMAN trained as an actor at the Bristol Old Vic Theatre School. He has acted and directed in England, Canada, and the USA. Currently he is an Head of Graduate Directing and Senior Acting Professor in the Professional Training Programme of the Department of Theatre, Film, and Creative Writing at the University of British Columbia. He also teaches regularly at the National Theatre School of Canada, Concordia University, Brigham Young University in both Provo and Hawaii, and is on the teaching faculty of professional workshops in Montreal, Toronto and Vancouver. He is associated with Shakespeare & Co. in Lenox; the Will Geer Theatre in Los Angeles; Bard on the Beach in Vancouver; Repercussion Theatre in Montreal; and has worked with the Stratford Festival, Canada, and Shakespeare Santa Cruz.

His ground breaking work in using the first printings of the Shakespeare texts in performance, on the rehearsal floor and in the classroom has lead to lectures at the Shakespeare Association of America and workshops at both the ATHE and VASTA, and grants/fellowships from the National Endowment of the Arts (USA), The Social Science and Humanities Research Council (Canada), and York University in Toronto.

His three collations of Shakespeare and music - *A Midsummer Nights Dream* (for three actors, chorus, and Orchestra); *If This Be Love* (for three actors, mezzo-soprano, and Orchestra); *The Four Seasons of Shakespeare and Vivaldi* (for two actors, violin soloist and Chamber Orchestra) - commissioned and performed by Bard On The Beach and The Vancouver Symphony Orchestra have been received with great public acclaim.

SHAKESPEARE'S
FIRST TEXTS
by Neil Freeman

"THE ACTOR'S BEST CHAMPION OF THE
FOLIO"   —Kristin Linklater
                author of *Freeing Shakespeare's Voice*

Neil Freeman provides students, scholars, theatre-lovers, and, most importantly, actors and directors, with a highly readable, illuminating, and indispensable guide to William Shakespeare's own first quill-inscribed texts — SHAKESPEARE'S FIRST TEXTS.

Four hundred years later, most of the grammatical and typographical information conveyed by this representation in Elizabethan type by the first play compositors has been lost. Or, rather, discarded, in order to conform to the new standards of usage. Granted, this permitted more readers access to Shakespeare's writing, but it also did away with some of Shakespeare himself.

ISBN 1-155783-335-4